WITH

[GIRL] FRIEND OF BILL

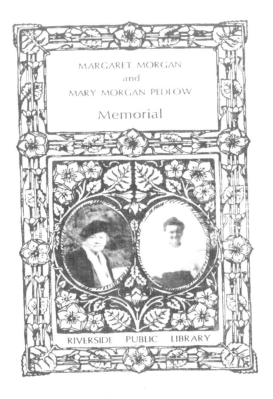

[GIRL]FRIEND OF BILL

12 Things
You Need to Know about
Dating Someone
in Recovery

KAREN NAGY

HAZELDEN®

Hazelden
Center City, Minnesota 55012
hazelden.org

LIBRARY OF CONGRESS CATALOGING-IN-PUBLICATION DATA

Nagy, Karen (Professor)
    Girlfriend of Bill : 12 things you need to know about dating
someone in recovery / Karen Nagy.
        pages   cm
        ISBN 978-1-61649-523-7 (pbk.) — ISBN 978-1-61649-527-5
(ebook)
    1. Recovering alcoholics. 2. Recovering addicts. 3. Dating
(Social customs) 4. Interpersonal relations. I. Title.
        HV5275.N34 2014
        362.29'13—dc23

                                                        2013044760

EDITOR'S NOTE
Some names, details, and circumstances have been changed
to protect the privacy of those mentioned in this publication.
This publication is not intended as a substitute for the
advice of health care professionals.
Alcoholics Anonymous, AA, the Big Book, the *Grapevine,*
and *AA Grapevine* are registered trademarks of
Alcoholics Anonymous World Services, Inc.

Hazelden offers a variety of information on addiction and
related areas. The views and interpretations expressed herein
are those of the author and are neither endorsed nor
approved by AA or any Twelve Step organization.

16 15 14   1 2 3 4 5 6

Cover design: Theresa Jaeger Gedig
Interior design: Cathy Spengler
Typesetting: BookMobile Design & Digital Publisher Services

For Reta and Ray,
my parents and biggest cheerleaders.
And for my faithful writing companions:
Dot, my "laptop cat," and
Annie and Lady Thiang, my angels.

Contents

Acknowledgments

First of all, I give thanks to my Higher Power for the perfect order in which this book came about. This was truly a God-job! Every day for four years, I envisioned that the right and perfect people and information would appear at the perfect time, and it happened. Thank you to all the good people at Hazelden who saw potential in the book, even in its early stages, and especially to my editor, Sid Farrar. Sid, I will be forever grateful to you for envisioning what this book could be. Thank you for your patience with me and your belief in the process. I am also grateful to you for assigning me to my amazingly talented and nurturing editor, Cynthia Orange. Cynthia, it is because of you that this book is what it is. You took me under your wing and showed me the voice the book needed. You are an awesome teacher, and I have learned so much. I feel like Eliza Doolittle with you as my Henry Higgins (but way nicer)! Your positive attitude, gentle guidance, and lighthearted touch made a rather daunting task actually enjoyable—often downright fun. You can "tweak my tweaks" anytime! Thank you for your friendship and support throughout the past several months.

I also thank my many friends and family members who have given me so much encouragement and support throughout the writing of this book. Special thanks to Chris and Mark: Chris, for your *long*time friendship; Mark, for our enlightening spiritual talks—and to both of you for sharing your journeys with me. To Bethany, Lisa and Bobby, Linda and Deb, David, Carol, Gail, Ellen, Dennis and Gwen, and many other friends who were my "ear" as the book was being written. To Karen and Allen for good interview suggestions. To Cindie, whose wisdom and strength give me such inspiration. Thank you to my colleague Debbie for the positive and encouraging writers' seminar that convinced me I could do this. Thank you to John for giving me good information on the process. Thanks to all my family members for their support and love, especially Mom and Dad, Kurt, Kyle, and "cuz" Collette.

To my dear friends in recovery, their partners, and my other friends who have been in a relationship with someone in recovery: I can't begin to express my gratitude for your bravery and candor in sharing your stories. Your names have been changed to protect your anonymity, but you know who you are. The book would not have been possible without you. Those of you in recovery have been such an inspiration to me in the way you continue to work your program, living your lives with honesty and integrity. I am especially grateful to my dear friend Mark, who made his transition shortly before the publication of this book. And finally, to all my friends who are partners of those in recovery: you have shown me that this *can* work. Thank you. This is your book.

Introduction

I've dated a number of guys in recovery. Maybe it's my personality type on the e-dating questionnaires; maybe it's my involvement in a type of church to which many in recovery go; or maybe it's my amazing ability to attract what I need to work on myself. (Patience, for instance, was never a virtue for me, but sometimes it's just what you need when you're in a relationship with someone in recovery.) At any rate, it's been a real learning experience.

When I first started dating Steve, I knew very little about him. I knew he was in recovery. I knew he attended Alcoholics Anonymous (AA) meetings every night, and I knew he was originally from my hometown area. He had a son from a previous marriage. He seemed like a lot of fun. He liked tennis and so do I, and I confess he was one handsome dude! But I did have questions about protocol while dating a person in recovery, and later, about why he did some of the things he did.

Steve was really funny and very generous, and he had a good heart. On the outside, he appeared to be perfectly normal. I figured, "Well, he isn't drinking, so everything must be okay, right?" Later on I realized that some of his behaviors that were odd, different, and sometimes hard to deal with were related to his addiction disorder. I had no idea that simply stopping drinking or using other drugs does not automatically prevent other addictive behaviors from occurring.

How I wished I'd been given a manual of sorts that explained it all! I found plenty of books for people in recovery, and some books for people already in a relationship with someone in recovery, but nothing specifically for someone who is new to such a relationship or who is thinking about dating someone in recovery.

I decided to write the book that I'd needed back when I first met Steve. It's based on my experiences dating people in recovery (I'll use "PIR" or "PIRs" throughout the book to represent a person in recovery or people in recovery) and my involvement with recovery groups. It includes interviews with others who shared their experiences about dating someone in recovery. How differently I would have handled many situations had I known that many of Steve's behaviors were common for those with an addiction disorder, that they were often predictable, and—with the right kind of support—that they were even manageable. On the other hand, had I known then what I now know about addiction and recovery, I may not have chosen to stay in that particular relationship as long as I did.

People in Twelve Step recovery often call themselves "friends of Bill," a reference to Bill W., the cofounder of AA. Being a "friend of Bill" is a sort of code for those in recovery who want to protect anonymity by not having to say they're in AA. For example, if a recovering alcoholic is at a party and they see someone else who's not drinking, they may eventually ask, "Are you a friend of Bill?" If the answer is yes, then both people know they are "in the program" and have something in common. When I dated someone who was seriously working a recovery program, that reality loomed so large in our relationship that it affected my actions and reactions to him and how we interacted as a couple. If he was a "friend of Bill," I felt like I had become, by extension, a "girlfriend of Bill," which explains this book's title. If your boyfriend or girlfriend is also in a recovery program, we also have something in common. So I say, "Welcome to the club."

If you're reading this book, you're probably dating or thinking about dating someone in recovery, and you want to learn more about recovery—especially how it may affect your dating experience and relationship with that person. I've included what I think are the twelve most important things to know or consider when dating someone in recovery from an addiction disorder. (I am specifically referring to alcoholism and drug addiction—I'm not including behavioral addictions like gambling or sex, although much of what I talk about probably applies to those too.)

1. Not all recovering people are alike
2. Addiction is a disease
3. Twelve Step recovery makes sense
4. Why some people call Steps Four through Ten the "relationship" Steps
5. Addictive behaviors don't magically disappear
6. How addictive traits can affect a relationship
7. Codependency is common, so healthy boundaries are essential

Of course, not all PIRs have all of the behaviors that are discussed in this book. Also keep in mind that you might meet your boyfriend or girlfriend after they've had many years of sobriety and have worked diligently on these behaviors. But no matter what stage they may be at in their recovery journey, perhaps learning about addiction and recovery can build a bridge to better understanding and open the door to more honest communication between the two of you.

When PIRs continue to "work their program"—which basically means going to Twelve Step meetings and applying the Steps in their lives (more about that later)—they also work to uncover parts of themselves that were hidden by their addictions. They usually learn to trust once again after having lost that ability during their drinking and using years, and most PIRs develop or deepen their spiritual lives, since that's at the heart of the Twelve Step program. Ideally, they are learning to be open to a new way of living. These skills can be wonderfully beneficial in a dating (or any) relationship. Also, many people in recovery are quite sensitive to others' feelings and needs because they've spent so much time in deep reflection and self-examination. "A sensitive man?" you women readers might be saying. "It's every woman's wish!" "A woman who doesn't try to 'fix' or change me?" you male readers might be thinking. "She'd be the perfect date!"

For me, it was important to know how my boyfriend Steve got to where he was, and this knowledge helped me learn about the biological, psychological, and social factors that make up addiction. I include that information in this book, and I also discuss what I've learned about recovery by giving an overview of AA, Narcotics Anonymous (NA), Al-Anon, Nar-Anon, and the practical wisdom of the Twelve Steps, including some popular slogans and affirmations. I hope you'll find, as I did, that learning about addiction and Twelve Step recovery can not only help you support your PIR, it can also help you help yourself.

There are stories throughout the book from people I know who are in recovery, from their significant others, and from books I've read. The partners of those in recovery gave me great tips based on how they've handled many of their PIRs' issues. The people I interviewed who are in recovery gave me firsthand information on what they were feeling and thinking as they dealt with these issues, and how they overcame many of them. I am grateful for their honesty, candor, and generosity in sharing their stories. I also include examples from my own relationships, including what I did to (gulp) enable my PIRs' behavior. I've changed names and any information that might identify these people to protect their anonymity.

I am a member of a church that is very open to Twelve Step programs, and I thought I was knowledgeable about what my friends in recovery went through—but I was not. So it's no surprise that I was unprepared to pursue a dating relationship with a person in recovery. I soon found out that when it came to dating these people, I was both a "wuss," in terms of being honest with my feelings, and a control freak. (Coincidentally, these can be addictive characteristics.) You, too, might find that you have your own set of issues that are eerily similar to those of your partner. If so, take heart—learning about addiction and recovery can provide a huge opportunity for your own personal growth, if you are brave enough to examine your own behaviors to see if they help or hinder your desire to build a strong relationship. My main goal in writing this book was to help people like you with that process.

Knowledge is both clarifying and empowering. I hope the information in this book will help you make healthy decisions about the person you are dating, and will also help both of you work together in a positive way. Blessings on your journey!

[1]

Not All
Recovering
People
Are Alike

IN THESE PAGES you'll read many stories about my friends who are in recovery, as well as stories about two of the five men I dated who were in recovery. I met many of these friends and one boyfriend in a "recovery friendly" church in which I was the music director, but since I wasn't in recovery myself, I didn't really know at the time what recovery meant. Their groups sounded more than a little mysterious to me. Was their recovery the same as recovering from a sprained ankle or from a cold? All I knew was that my friends were following something called the Twelve Steps, and that these Steps were so popular that they were even included in some of our non-recovery church programs.

What I found out was that being in recovery from an addictive substance is not at all like recovering from a knee injury, hip surgery, or a broken heart. I discovered I wasn't the only one who was confused. For a lot of years, even many people in the field of addiction studies were of the opinion that recovery from alcohol and other drugs simply meant being abstinent—getting "clean and sober." But in recent years, research has shown that effective recovery includes much more than abstinence.

Here is the definition of *recovery* that came from a panel convened by the Betty Ford Center, a well-respected leader in the recovery movement:

> *Recovery from substance dependence is a voluntarily maintained lifestyle characterized by sobriety, personal health and citizenship.*[1]

In this definition, *sobriety* means abstinence from alcohol and all other nonprescribed mood-altering drugs. *Personal health* is about an improved quality of life that includes physical health, psychological health, and independence, as well as spirituality—a sense of something bigger than you that gives life meaning. And *citizenship* refers to living with regard and respect for others.

This definition of recovery strikes me as holistic and positive. And the reference to recovery being "voluntary" is always a good reminder to me that, although we can support, befriend, and love them, people in recovery (PIRs) are ultimately responsible for their own recovery.

People in recovery from alcohol and other drugs come from all walks of life and backgrounds. Some of them (the "friends of Bill" I mentioned in the introduction to this book) attend Alcoholics Anonymous (AA) or Narcotics Anonymous (NA), and follow a recovery program that is based on the Twelve Steps—established principles and practices that offer a blueprint for living a healthy, drug- and alcohol-free life. In addition to AA and NA, there are Twelve Step groups that focus on a particular drug, such as Marijuana Anonymous, Pills Anonymous, and Cocaine Anonymous (which is open to all people who desire to be clean and sober regardless of their drug of choice). In addition, there are support groups for people with co-occurring addiction and mental health disorders: Double Trouble in Recovery, Dual Diagnosis Anonymous, and Dual Recovery Anonymous.

Although I focus on Twelve Step recovery in this book, your PIR may attend a recovery group that offers alternatives to the Twelve Steps, such as SMART Recovery, Women for Sobriety, or Secular Organizations for Sobriety. Some PIRs prefer support groups that are made up of people from their same occupation, such as Physicians Serving Physicians, Peer Assistance Program for Nurses, Accountants Concerned for Accountants, Lawyers Concerned for Lawyers, Dentists Concerned for Dentists, or Pharmacists Helping Pharmacists. Other PIRs have found the ongoing support they need in groups at their church, at their synagogue or temple, in their mental health peer support or therapy group, or in a support group based on a nonreligious spiritual path.

PIRs can range from highly educated to barely educated, from rich to poor, from young to old. They can come from seemingly normal families or totally dysfunctional families. They can be male or female, be of different races, be heterosexual or from the LGBT (lesbian, gay, bisexual, transgender) community. Some PIRs are very religious and active in their faith communities. Others might consider themselves spiritual but not religious. Some might be atheists or agnostics. In other words, there is no single way to categorize PIRs. They are as varied as the general population.

You may have heard the old adage "You can't judge a book by its cover." As I mentioned earlier, even a PIR wouldn't know at first, or even second, glance if someone they meet is recovering from an addictive disorder. How much easier it would be if the stunningly beautiful woman you're interested in had a "Recovering Alcoholic" tattoo on her right arm, or if the cute guy you flirted with at the gym wore a "Recovering Meth Addict" tee shirt. PIRs can be charming and smart, quick to have a funny retort, very social, and have many other attractive traits. I laugh out loud at some of the witty comments my friend Sandy comes up with. On the other hand, PIRs can have some downright irritating traits: for example, my friend Don can be a walking wave of negativity. Everyone is different.

I have many friends in recovery, all of them with unique issues and personalities. I've also dated five men in various stages of recovery. Three of these men were not following their program, and I decided not to date them any further. Mike, three years sober, stopped going to meetings, declaring, "Hey, I know I'm not going to drink or use again, so I don't need that stuff anymore." Another one, Pat, decided that beer didn't really affect him as much as pot did, so, even though he wasn't smoking pot, he'd occasionally have a beer or two. He also had a pretty loose lifestyle, living with whatever woman he was currently dating and not accepting responsibility for his children. I knew right away that these guys weren't for me, and I hope they have not *relapsed* (started drinking or using again—more about that later).

Because you've read this far, I assume you're dating or thinking about dating someone in recovery. Perhaps your PIR attends AA or NA meetings, maybe even every night. If they are going to AA, they will most likely be reading and following *Alcoholics Anonymous,* the basic text of AA, more commonly referred to as the Big Book. The Big Book was first published in 1939 by the two men who founded AA to show other alcoholics "precisely how we have recovered."[2]

Or your PIR might be attending NA. The Fellowship of Narcotics Anonymous was formed in the 1950s when some people who were addicted to drugs other than alcohol (or in addition to alcohol) realized they could benefit from their own support group. In 1962, they published their own basic text, *Narcotics Anonymous.* It too uses the Twelve Steps as a basis of its recovery program, and today there are thousands of NA meetings in the United States and in many foreign countries.

The first chapters of both the Big Book and *Narcotics Anonymous* describe how their programs work and include details on the Twelve Steps. In the latter part of each book, one can find many stories about people in recovery and how they came to their recovery. What an array of personalities and circumstances!

The stories reflect the variety of people in recovery. For example, in the Big Book, an African American physician who lost almost everything to alcohol tells how he became sober and helped start the first black AA group.[3] A stay-at-home mother describes how she hid her bottles in clothes hampers and dresser drawers in her home.[4] A Native American woman with a troubled past tells how she was rescued by a caring "angel" of a woman in a Laundromat.[5]

In *Narcotics Anonymous,* an Orthodox Jew tells how recovery helped him forge a new relationship with his Higher Power.[6] (The concept of a Higher Power will be discussed more fully in chapter 3.) A Kenyan boy who lived on the streets talks about how he felt like he had finally found a home in NA.[7] A Mexican woman tells how she walked through the doors of NA and was treated with more love and respect than she'd ever had before.[8]

You may already know some people who attend Twelve Step meetings, or you may be new to the world of recovery. If you become involved with a PIR, you will most likely get to know a couple of your partner's friends who will have similar stories. That happened to me, and I also met a variety of other PIRs on my own over the years. Some of these folks have become longtime friends to me, and each of them has their own unique stories.

One dear friend is Mark, who is from a Puerto Rican family that settled in New York. He's been clean and sober nine years now. He has chronic depression and struggles sometimes with balancing his prescribed medications. He's sensitive, kind, and spiritual, and I treasure our friendship.

Denise was a professional actress in New York, but returned to her native North Carolina for recovery and family purposes. She is hysterically funny and enormously talented. She also battles depression.

Joe was a former teacher who became an addictions counselor after he got sober. He died recently, and scores of folks he had helped attended his memorial service. One young lady tearfully claimed, "Joe saved my life."

Josh, a gay Cuban American, was a cocaine addict. He's been sober for fifteen years, works in management for a very successful not-for-profit company, and occasionally still sings professionally with his God-given glorious voice.

I'm friends with several couples as well. Seth has been happily married to Pam (who is not a PIR) for thirty-six years. He is a former businessman who was addicted to drugs and alcohol. After getting sober, he earned a master's degree in psychology. They are now retired and are active in the adult community in which they live. They are two of the most spiritual people I know.

Frank and Donna are two of Mark's best friends. Frank is a PIR; Donna is not, but she came from abusive circumstances as a child. They are examples of yin and yang in a relationship, as they both support each other and contribute their own unique strengths.

Paul and Sandy are both PIRs who met in a recovery program. Both are very active in the recovery community in my town. Paul has established and manages several recovery centers in the area. Paul and Sandy are shining examples of two people who successfully live and work their recovery programs.

Although I speak admirably of these people who are my friends and inspirations, it is essential for you to know that they have not always had an easy time of it in their recovery. They are continually working on the issues that led to their drinking and using in the first place. Several of them have had at least one relapse. Their experiences taught me that even people in long-term recovery know that they must always be vigilant in their sobriety.

My friends in recovery taught me the difference between the words *recovered* and *recovering.* Although many of these PIRs might say they "recovered" their lives, their families, their relationships with friends, or their spirituality when they stopped drinking or using, most of them do not consider themselves as recovered when it comes to their addictions. They may have learned how to manage their lives, but they tell me they will always be "recover*ing*" addicts or alcoholics because addiction is a tough, chronic, and potentially fatal disease from which one never fully recovers.

It is not always easy to have a relationship with someone in recovery. Many PIRs have seen their relationships fail because of their addictive habits. I struggled with several of my former boyfriends' issues, and even if I knew then what I know today, it still wouldn't have been easy for me. My hope is that as you read about addiction and recovery in this book and learn how I and others handled (or didn't handle) our relationships, your own journey will be a little smoother.

[2]

Addiction
Is a Disease

I WONDERED ABOUT ALCOHOLISM and drug addiction long before I dated guys in recovery. My mom told me stories about what happened when she was a young girl; stories of her father coming home from the bars in a drunken rage. Mom would hide under the kitchen table to escape her dad and his tirades. My grandfather died of a cerebral hemorrhage when my mom was just seven years old. She suspected it was related to his drinking, and her stories made me wonder about the dividing line between having a drink or two and being an alcoholic.

I have since learned that the American Psychiatric Association has classified alcoholism and other drug addictions as diseases, falling under substance use disorders in its *Diagnostic and Statistical Manual of Mental Disorders,* 5th edition *(DSM-5)*—the diagnostic reference book used by professionals who treat addiction. In researching this, I found a very good online booklet, *Drugs, Brains, and Behavior: The Science of Addiction,* by the National Institute on Drug Abuse (NIDA), which gives this definition of addiction:

> Addiction is defined as a chronic, relapsing brain disease
> that is characterized by compulsive drug seeking and use,
> despite harmful consequences. It is considered a brain
> disease because drugs change the brain—they change
> its structure and how it works. These brain changes can be
> long lasting, and can lead to the harmful behaviors seen
> in people who abuse drugs.[9]

So my grandfather had a disease, a disease that did not
fully manifest until he began drinking. My grandma said that
when she first married him he never drank; it was "those
guys down at the plant that got him going to the bars after
work, and once he started drinking he couldn't stop."

Back in those days, which was just about the time that
the Big Book was first published, many people believed that
an alcoholic or addict merely lacked the willpower to say no
to the next drink or fix. It was Dr. William Silkworth—the
doctor who treated Bill W. and other alcoholics—who wrote
in "The Doctor's Opinion" in the Big Book, "the action of
alcohol on these chronic alcoholics is a manifestation of an
allergy; that the phenomenon of craving is limited to this
class and never occurs in the average temperate drinker."[10]

What the doctor called an allergy we now call a brain
disease, based on the wealth of research that has been done
since Dr. Silkworth had that remarkable insight.

This explained a lot—it helped me better understand
why some of us can have a drink or two and be done with
it; why others might smoke one joint or even experiment
with a powerful drug like heroin and not get hooked; and
others can't control how much they drink or use, no matter what the consequences may be. The brain of an addict
is different from that of a non-addict. It can tolerate more

and more alcohol or other drugs until the person loses control and becomes addicted.

I remember a time years ago when I was out at a restaurant with a group of my theater friends after a show. My friend Rob was with us, and, while the rest of us ordered wine or beer, he had a Coke. I had known at that point that he was a PIR—he was very open with us about it. I remember feeling sorry for him, thinking how hard it must be for him, wondering why I could have a couple of drinks and he couldn't. I wondered what it was in his background that made him susceptible to this. I confess that I thought of him as different, maybe even a little weird. And it made me somewhat uncomfortable to be with him while the rest of us were drinking and having a good time. I wondered why he kept talking about AA and why he still had to go to meetings—at that point, he'd been sober about ten years. I like to think that I was being open-minded and sympathetic toward Rob at the time, but I admit I was a little judgmental. I still didn't know much about addiction. At the time, I thought it was a moral failing or a weakness of will, but I now know it's a brain disease—a chronic condition that Rob has to monitor for the rest of his life.

Now I understand more about PIRs and what happens in the brains of those who are addicted to alcohol or other drugs. The brain is made up of about 100 billion nerve cells (neurons) that are separated by tiny gaps called *synapses.* Like a miniature electric circuit, the neurons pass messages back and forth across these synapses by using chemicals called *neurotransmitters.* Because drugs are also chemicals, they affect the brain by interfering with the way neurons send, receive, and process information.

Some drugs, such as marijuana, can artificially activate neurons. The drug's chemical structure resembles that of a natural neurotransmitter, so it activates the neurons by "fooling" them. Other drugs, such as cocaine, can cause the neurons to release abnormally large amounts of natural neurotransmitters, producing a greatly amplified message, similar to someone screaming into your ear instead of whispering.

Most mood-altering drugs target the brain's reward system by flooding the circuit with dopamine. Dopamine is the "feel good" chemical that is present in regions of the brain that register emotion and feelings of pleasure. When this system that normally rewards our natural behaviors gets overstimulated, it produces the euphoric high that drug addicts seek, and teaches them to keep drinking and drugging.

This all makes more sense to me now. I didn't realize how alcohol and other drugs could actually take over someone's brain. I did know about dopamine because I'm a runner and I'm used to getting that "runner's high" many runners experience after about twenty minutes, but I didn't understand how dopamine and drugs interact. Now I can see how someone who is susceptible to addiction can get hooked on drugs after they begin experimenting with them. It's about brain chemistry, not a lack of self-control.

Some addictive drugs can release two to ten times the amount of dopamine that we would get naturally, and they can do it almost immediately, especially if the drug is smoked or injected. The immediacy of such a powerful reward makes drug users want to use again and again. And if they keep taking the drug, their brains adjust to this high level of dopamine by producing less of it. As a result, addicts can feel energy-depleted, depressed, and unable to enjoy things that used to give them pleasure. When this happens, they need to take drugs just to get their dopamine level back up to normal. Then they have to take even larger amounts of their drug than they previously did in order to create the dopamine high. This is known as *tolerance*—their bodies have become used to the drug, and they now crave more. Continued abuse of drugs can lead to addiction, which, as NIDA says, can drive an addict to seek out and take drugs compulsively.[11] This in turn erodes the addict's self-control and ability to make sound decisions—no matter what the consequences may be. For some alcoholics and addicts who might be predisposed due to genetics and their brain chemistry, addiction can seemingly kick in with the first drink or hit. A common expression you'll hear from these people in reaction to that first high is, "Where have you been all my life?"

Mood-altering drugs also can damage other parts of the body if people use them long enough. Alcohol not only damages brain cells, but can also harm organs such as the heart, liver, and pancreas. Inhalants are toxic to nerve cells and may damage or destroy them either in the brain or in other parts of the nervous system. Marijuana can affect short-term memory. And any time addicts use a needle to inject opiates, such as heroin or meth (methamphetamine), they put themselves at risk for HIV/AIDS and hepatitis C.

Over time, consistent use of alcohol and other drugs can change the brain's chemistry. At first, the damage is acute and temporary. But with prolonged use of drugs or alcohol, there can often be permanent damage. Chronic alcoholics and drug addicts often have difficulty solving problems or remembering things. They might have trouble communicating or understanding what they read or hear, and even their movements and eyesight can be affected.

If people with addiction disorders need mood-altering drugs in their systems just to feel "normal," it makes sense that their brains and bodies can go through some dramatic changes when they stop using. Withdrawal symptoms vary in severity and length, depending on the drug and the degree to which a person was addicted to it. But, no matter how long or how mild or severe the symptoms may be, going through withdrawal and learning to live without the drug that their minds and bodies continue to "tell" them they need at all costs, is a big adjustment for PIRs. That is why they are cautioned not to date in their first year of recovery.

Some alcoholics and drug addicts can get violently ill if they try to stop using on their own. Many of them go to a detoxification (detox) center at a hospital or clinic before entering treatment (or in the treatment center if it's available) because they need a safe place where they can go through withdrawal under medical supervision. While others don't need a detox center, they still need enough time and a safe place to go through withdrawal before they can fully concentrate on recovery.

It can take months for an addict's body to adjust to abstinence. Aches and pains are common in withdrawal, and so are digestive problems that can include constipation, diarrhea, and loss of appetite. Some people might have difficulty thinking clearly or have memory problems. Others might have trouble with physical movement and coordination. Sleep disorders can be a huge problem for those who struggle to quit drinking and drugging, and for some PIRs, insomnia never goes away.

Stress can be another constant companion for those in withdrawal and recovery. Some PIRs say they have to constantly monitor their stress levels because they know how stress can increase a number of symptoms that can lead to relapse. My friend Josh said he had to be very mindful of stress for the first three years until he gradually learned how to handle it. Being aware of this mind-set is very important for someone who is dating a PIR. Knowing when something might be stressful for your PIR helps you do what you can to avoid those situations, and makes it easier for you and your PIR to develop strategies to deal with stress if a situation can't be avoided. (More about this in chapter 10.)

If you do not come from the realm of addiction, reading all this information may be quite overwhelming, especially if you've just started to date someone in recovery from addiction. The good news is that addiction can be managed successfully, and studies have shown that with long-term abstinence, a person's brain has a remarkable ability to recover, or at least partially recover. There are also effective withdrawal, anti-craving, and maintenance medications available for those who might need them. And there are proven mental health and counseling therapies to help PIRs rid their bodies and minds of the toxic presence of the drugs that have overtaken their lives. These various forms of treatment can counteract addiction's powerful effect on the brain and enable PIRs to regain control of their lives, setting the stage for further recovery. PIRs with severe addictions or co-occurring disorder problems might need to stay in an inpatient treatment facility for a time because they need additional mental health and medical services, including medications for conditions such as anxiety or depression. This inpatient treatment is sometimes followed up with a stay at a halfway house or other residential treatment facility, giving those with severe addiction or co-occurring disorder problems more time to slowly enter the world of ongoing recovery.

You may be wondering, as I did, why someone would abuse drugs in the first place—how could anyone choose to do something like this to their brain and body? People don't set out to become addicted to drugs or alcohol. Many alcoholics and addicts—like many of us—experimented with abusive substances as teenagers. Some (like many of us) started using drugs or alcohol to feel good, to lessen anxiety, to enhance performance in sports or in the classroom, or to just fit in "because others were doing it." The difference is we could quit when things got out of hand. Someone with an addiction disorder can't do that.

My friend Frank was a timid child, hypersensitive and often picked on. He says he was often terrified and lived in fear, so he began to smoke pot in the fifth grade to "escape." He started drinking alcohol in sixth grade.

Seth said he always had low self-esteem and never felt like he belonged. He began drinking heavily in college when he was eighteen, and eventually started using pot, hash, and mescaline on a regular basis.

Josh also had low self-esteem. He described the stigma of growing up gay in a Cuban American community and how he developed self-worth issues. He said he started drinking at age fifteen to "numb reality."

No single factor determines whether or not a person

will get addicted. I've learned that the overall risk for addiction is a combination of genetic makeup, the environment in which a person lives, and their psychological disposition. This is why some researchers refer to addiction as a "bio-psycho-social" disease. Others might say addiction is a disease that affects the body, mind, and spirit—often a combination of all three areas. A person can inherit a susceptibility to addiction but may not develop a problem if they have a stable environment and healthy mental attitude and don't start abusing alcohol or other drugs. However, they are still at high risk for addiction if anything in the other areas throws them off-balance.

The body of someone who is susceptible to addiction does not react in the same way to alcohol or other drugs as the body of someone who is not susceptible. Addiction is often called "a family disease," and research has shown that those who have a genetic tendency to alcoholism metabolize alcohol differently from those who don't have this tendency. Numerous studies that involve children of alcoholics show that they have a greater chance of developing this disease than the children of non-alcoholics—especially sons of alcoholics. What about environmental factors? During adolescence, even children without genetic risk factors can be swayed by friends and acquaintances to try alcohol or other drugs. As I learned from friends in recovery, pressure to fit in, academic failure, or poor social skills can also put a child at risk.

The home environment is another big factor when it comes to alcohol and other drug use. Children from dysfunctional families can grow up at opposite ends of the spectrum—some might drink or use drugs abusively, while some won't touch alcohol or other drugs. They might become addicts who are attracted to other addicts. This attraction is especially likely for children who come from an addictive household, because this is what they know, what they've seen, and how they learned to cope. They "speak the same language," the language of addiction. My friend Grace came from an alcoholic family and ended up marrying a PIR with a personality profile much like her father's.

I wish I had known when I began dating PIRs that children from addictive households have a difficult time knowing what is "normal." One minute they are the child, the next minute they are the "adult," as their parents likewise shift from "adult" to "child" in their behavior. There is a sense of dread and doom from living in a crisis-based family that often carries into adulthood.

If children come from a type of family that shames and blames, they can be especially vulnerable to addiction. Shaming families learn to bring others down in order to build themselves up. They can be manipulative while pretending to be helpful or honest. They often demand perfection, pushing their children to have perfect grades even if the child brings home just one B+. As a result, many such children learn that they are never good enough. They sometimes develop a secret life, or a mistrust of people (a dangerous tendency for addicts), or they might believe that if people "really knew" them, they wouldn't like them. In adulthood, they may feel defensive if anyone points out a mistake they made. They might become perfectionists themselves, and perfect candidates for addiction.

People with mental disorders are also at greater risk for drug and alcohol abuse and addiction than the general population. I can understand this well, because I currently have two very good friends whose sons are living with mental disorders while also battling drug addiction.

One of these, my young friend Jason, was diagnosed with obsessive-compulsive disorder (OCD) in junior high school; in high school he had a schizoaffective diagnosis (he exhibited symptoms of both schizophrenia and bipolar disorder) and also had severe anxiety and depression. He began abusing drugs and alcohol in high school. Today, eight years later, his most recent diagnosis is severe attention deficit hyperactivity disorder (ADHD) together with bipolar disorder and alcohol addiction. He has been sober from pot for two years, but continues to relapse with alcohol.

My close friend Mark had a miserable childhood—his mother was mentally unstable and abusive, and his father left the family when Mark was nine. He had four younger brothers and took care of them because his mother couldn't. Mark says he realized he was depressed at age seven. He began drinking at age eleven. His mother had beer in the refrigerator, and she'd let him and his brothers drink it. He later got into drugs and increased his drinking, both to help him escape from the low self-esteem of his childhood and to ease the pain of his depression, which grew increasingly worse. It's common for people to try to "medicate" the pain of emotional disorders with alcohol or other drugs. As with Mark, it can feel like it's easier to use drugs than to try to deal with a mental health problem. Everything eventually centered on his using and drinking. Today, many years later, his latest diagnosis is bipolar disorder with severe depression. He takes prescription medication for the depression and has been sober for nine years.

Many PIRs I know talk about the stigma of addiction, and how hard it was to admit they had a problem when they felt like they were being judged or looked down upon. Now it's easier for me to understand what they mean when they talk about stigma and to empathize with them. When drugs take over people's lives, everything changes. They begin to develop other addictive behavior patterns and start thinking like an addict. As I discovered when I entered a relationship with a PIR, they can carry some of these patterns and traits into their sobriety. But knowing that addiction is a disease has helped me to confront and get over my past prejudices about alcoholics and drug addicts, and to better understand why they might think, act, and react the way they do. Now I think of PIRs in the same way I think of my friend Toni, who has had diabetes since she was thirteen, or my student Karrie, who has lupus. Addicts and alcoholics also have a chronic disease that can be managed successfully—just like Toni and Karrie are handling their diseases. Most of my friends who are PIRs are managing their diseases, in large part, by attending and following Twelve Step programs such as AA and NA.

[3]

Twelve Step Recovery Makes Sense

WHEN I MET STEVE and found out he was a "friend of Bill," I nodded knowingly, stayed cool, and acted like I really knew what he was talking about. I had heard people talk about recovery groups at church and had taken a class about success that used the Twelve Steps as a format. I could even quote a couple of Steps. But I've learned there is a big difference between hearing about something and really understanding it. At first I thought Twelve Step recovery was something reserved for "them"—the millions of people all over the world who can't manage their drinking or drugging or eating or gambling or other behaviors that have become out of control. It certainly didn't pertain to *me* or *my* life. Little did I know.

As I emphasized earlier, recovery is more than just abstinence. The Betty Ford Center's definition in chapter 1 refers to recovery as a "voluntarily maintained lifestyle," meaning that it is an ongoing process and a commitment to good health in all areas: physical, emotional, mental, and spiritual. It is in recovery that addicts uncover the parts of themselves that addiction took away.

Recovery groups used to be called "self-help" groups,

but now most people prefer to describe them as mutual-help or peer support groups, which makes more sense to me. Although PIRs are ultimately responsible for their own sobriety and choices, in a recovery program they learn to reach out to others and to no longer isolate themselves in the world of addiction. They learn to work through their problem areas. They learn to control their urges to immediately seek pleasure, power, or control. As they focus their lives on continuous self-examination and meaning, they learn coping skills and how to live in the moment. Most PIRs became used to living life in the fast lane. In recovery, they learn how to move more slowly, thoughtfully, and intentionally. It's like the African proverb I once heard: "If you want to go fast, go alone. If you want to go far, go together." The road from the insanity of addiction to the serenity of recovery can be long and challenging, but the journey is made easier with traveling companions.

"One day at a time" is a popular phrase in Twelve Step recovery groups. Day by day, PIRs begin to reclaim their true selves. Even though PIRs are not drinking or using, the addiction disorder is still present in them, and they are constantly monitoring themselves so as not to slip back into addictive behaviors like isolation, secrecy, negative thinking, and making excuses. They also learn to deal with other things common to addiction disorders such as distorted thinking (most commonly denial), compulsion, dishonesty, fear, resentment, selfishness, low self-worth, low frustration tolerance, and oversensitivity—all of which will be discussed in more detail in upcoming chapters.

PIRs come to recovery in many ways. Sometimes worried loved ones make the first move by doing an "intervention," when they express their concerns about someone's addictive behavior and its impact on everyone involved, and encourage the person to go into treatment. The first time I ever heard of the term *intervention* was when my friend told me about how her family had sat her mother down to tell her how they felt about her drinking and how it was affecting the whole family. It was a big deal, for them and for her, because everyone had been in denial for way too long. They had received guidance from an addictions counselor beforehand so they would know what to do and say. They learned that an intervention was about addressing a person's behavior, not beating up on them or shaming them. They told her they loved her and that they would help her in any way they could. The family insisted that the mom get help, and she agreed to be taken to a treatment center they had lined up. In treatment, she learned about AA, and she still goes to her meetings faithfully.

Other PIRs might be in recovery because they had one too many DUIs (driving under the influence), or they were arrested for stealing, domestic abuse, or some other behavior related to their addiction disorder and a court ordered them to go to AA or NA as a condition of their parole. Some PIRs might discover AA or NA in prison. And some simply enter recovery on their own. They may have an inkling they have a problem, attend an AA or NA meeting out of curiosity, and then make the decision to give sobriety—and recovery—a chance. Or they may be "sick and tired of being sick and tired" as I've heard PIRs say, and have finally hit bottom—when the consequences of drinking and drugging have become so great that a person is ready to get help.

Although there are many paths to and types of recovery,

this book focuses on the one I came to know the best, the Twelve Step program. A Twelve Step program adapts the Twelve Steps of Alcoholics Anonymous to fit the particular needs of a mutual-help group, such as AA, NA, or Al-Anon. The Twelve Steps were formulated by the founders of AA as a way to thoroughly and systematically bring oneself to a healthy and meaningful place without the crutch of alcohol or other drugs.

A Twelve Step program can seem mysterious to someone who is outside the program looking in. If you are dating a PIR and they begin to talk about "redoing" Step Four, or how hard it was to "do" a proper Step Nine, or they mention concepts like a "Higher Power," "powerlessness," or "making amends," you might be baffled or worry they've joined some weird New Age or religious cult. But, never fear! As I discovered, a Twelve Step program is one of the most practical approaches to healthy living ever developed. Trust, acceptance, love, goodwill, and forgiveness are key elements in a Twelve Step program—just as they are important elements of any healthy relationship. What's scary about that?

I cannot begin to describe what a difference AA and NA have made in my PIR friends' lives. Many of them have turned their lives around with the help of these groups and consider their group a second home. And more people worldwide have successfully abstained from alcohol and other drugs or managed their addictive behaviors with Twelve Step programs than with any other kind of treatment.

At the time I met my boyfriend, Steve, he primarily attended AA meetings at a place close to where he lived, but he also knew of and attended other meetings in our town, depending on where he was when he got off work and what his plans were for that night. I wish now that we'd talked more about AA and the meetings. I also wish that I'd gone along with him to the meetings that were open to non-PIRs. (Ironically, it was after we broke up that I started going to open meetings in a church activity room not far from where I live.)

I have to say that, at times, I was mystified about what went on in these meetings. I also was, I hate to admit, a little paranoid and even jealous about all the time Steve spent at them. What went on? Were they talking about us non-PIRs? What was the magic ingredient that made the PIRs keep going back? Why were these damn Steps so important?

A PIR friend of mine said that her early experience in Twelve Step recovery was like being embraced in a big cocoon of love and support that comes from the fellowship of others who have been in the exact place she, as a newcomer to sobriety, had been in. "It gave me such hope to be with them and see how they'd come through it," she told me. "I'd leave a meeting thinking, 'If they can do it, maybe I can too.'" Although my boyfriend didn't talk about AA much at first, he did tell me he felt that same sense of relief when he first started attending meetings. He talked about the empathy, the understanding, and the love he felt in those meeting rooms. I remembered his description some time later when I read this passage from the Big Book about recovery groups: "I found my tribe, the social architecture that fulfills my every need for camaraderie and conviviality. I learned how to live."[12] That, I think, is the magic ingredient: tribe. PIRs keep going to meetings because the meetings and the people who attend them offer them the support and guidance they need to live a better life, one day at a time.

So it is very important that your PIR attend frequent meetings. For someone dating a PIR, the PIR's commitment to go to a number of meetings during the week may not make sense at first. You might even experience some jealousy, as I did, over your PIR seeming to spend more time in AA or NA than with you. It's important to remember that sobriety is a PIR's first priority, and going to meetings is a critical part of staying sober for most PIRs. If you find that this is a problem for you, you might want to talk about this with your PIR and let them know that spending time together is important to you. Let them know you'd like to explore ways to do that without them jeopardizing their sobriety or trying to limit the number of meetings they need to attend. With healthy, respectful, and honest communication, couples can come to a mutual understanding about time together and time apart. Your PIR's meeting time might be a great opportunity for you to catch up with friends, get back to that novel you've been reading, or do something else just for you.

PIRs will also be communicating frequently with others in the program. They "got sober" (as my PIR used to say) with these friends—they are each other's support system and lifeline. They are also being counseled to help others, to spread the word about recovery to others in the Twelfth Step (the Steps are listed later in this chapter). They may be asked to speak about their experience at prisons or recovery centers. It is essential that you understand the importance of meetings, and that you are supportive and factor in time in your relationship for your PIR to attend them. In early recovery many PIRs have the need and desire to attend "ninety meetings in ninety days," another reason

they're discouraged from striking up a new dating relationship during their first year of recovery. After they're more
secure in their recovery, this intensity lessens. Most PIRs
find a comfortable "home group" that meets weekly. One
guy I dated was eighteen years sober, and attended meetings less regularly, when he felt the need.

Narcotics Anonymous literature refers to the "triangle
of self-obsession" that is present in an addiction disorder. Resentment, anger, and fear make up this unhealthy
triangle—emotions that affect both addicts and those close
to them. In NA and AA, PIRs are given a new set of tools to
help them replace resentment with acceptance, anger with
love, and fear with faith and new hope. The point is, try to
be open to your PIR's need to go to meetings—your relationship will be the better for it.

There are several types of AA and NA meetings. The
meetings will either be closed (with only AA or NA members in attendance) or open. You don't have to be an alcoholic or addict to attend an open meeting; many people
go to an open meeting to get information about addiction,
or they might attend because they think they may have a
problem but aren't ready to commit to a recovery program.
Meetings are often held in activity rooms of churches or
other pretty simple settings because of the cheap rent and
flexible hours. Depending on the size of the city, meetings
can generally be found at practically any time of day or evening. Your PIR may be attending these meetings for the rest
of his or her life, so it is important for you to know what
goes on in these meetings that seem to be drawing your PIR
away from you so often.

Most Twelve Step meetings generally follow the AA

meeting format. At "speaker meetings," a volunteer from the group or a guest from another group usually tells their personal story, called "qualifying," or sometimes a speaker talks about one of the Steps or a theme from the Big Book or NA basic text. "Big Book meetings" focus on reading selections and group discussions about a topic or section from the Big Book. At "topic meetings," a member might want to discuss something that pertains to the group, such as sponsorship (discussed later in this chapter) or emotional sobriety (discussed in an upcoming chapter).

At "Step meetings," a volunteer member gives a short talk and leads a discussion about one of the Twelve Steps or one of the Twelve Traditions, a set of principles and values that guide group behavior. Anonymity (the understanding that the identities of members who attend a Twelve Step group will be protected) plays a big role in the Traditions. That's why members introduce themselves by their first names only ("Hi, I'm Bill and I'm an alcoholic [or 'addict' in NA]"), sometimes adding the initial of their last name, as in "Bill W." Those who attend meetings agree that "what is said in the room stays in the room." This knowledge builds trust and encourages complete honesty among those who attend because they don't need to be afraid of having their secrets shared without their permission. Understanding the necessity for and value of anonymity at meetings lessened my paranoia and helped explain why my PIR didn't talk much about what went on at them. Eventually, when we realized it's possible to talk about the *program* without talking about the *people*, I felt less threatened and he felt less pressured to reveal confidences.

While every meeting has its own personality and will

vary depending on the type of meeting it is, they usually follow a similar pattern, with volunteer leaders, or "trusted servants," facilitating the meeting. I recently attended an open meeting at the invitation of my friend Bob, and this was the order of the evening:

- preliminary coffee and social time
- non-AA announcements
- welcoming of newcomers
- Serenity Prayer, spoken in unison
- reading of the Twelve Steps, usually by different people
- reading of some of the Twelve Traditions
- reading of a "theme" for the night
- featured speaker
- audience comments/testimonies
- AA business
- closing circle and Lord's Prayer
- putting away chairs, cleaning up
- possibly going out for coffee afterward

Many PIRs will tell you that a good NA or AA meeting will leave them with something to think about afterward. As one PIR friend put it, "I've been going to NA meetings for over fifteen years, and I still learn new things that help me stay on the right track or help me know if I'm getting off track." I strongly encourage those of you dating a PIR to go to an open meeting with (or without) your partner. It can help lessen that sense of mystery or suspicion you may be feeling about AA or NA.

Your PIR will probably have a sponsor, and if your PIR has been in the program for a while, they may even be a sponsor. A sponsor is an AA or NA member (same sex as the PIR if they're straight, opposite sex if the PIR is gay or lesbian) with at least a couple of years of sobriety who is well grounded in recovery. The PIR chooses this sponsor to help guide them through the program, and to be a mentor and confidant. Especially if the "sponsee" is fairly new to the program, they will be in contact quite a bit with their sponsor. My boyfriend Steve's sponsor was involved to a great extent at first, and then only occasionally, when the need arose. Personally, I think he should have been on Steve's case about a lot more issues than he was, but Steve didn't exactly share everything that was going on, either. What I did discover was that sometimes the sponsors are as challenged as those they sponsor. Everyone in AA and NA is working on their own issues—sponsors are no exception. Sponsors aren't professional counselors; they are just laypeople, learning the best they can how to have a sober lifestyle. They do this and other service work to stay sober themselves, not to set themselves up as an authority or expert. A good sponsor/ sponsee relationship is like having a good teacher for algebra class—they help the PIR "get it." They illuminate for the PIR what in their life is working and not working, and help them deal successfully with their issues. In the end, though, a sponsor isn't responsible for what their sponsees do with the information and support they provide; it's up to each PIR to put something into the program if they want to get something out of it. My friend Seth shared with me that he had a wonderful sponsor who helped him move to a better position in his place of work that wasn't so stress-filled. Seth's sponsor also helped him work through the Twelve Steps, carefully and with honesty.

The Twelve Steps are basically a guide for PIRs that helps them live their lives authentically in order to keep growing in a positive and healthy direction. Although the Twelve Steps are definitely spiritual, they are not religious. Anyone can adapt the Steps to their personal beliefs, whether they are Jewish, Christian, Muslim, Buddhist, practice Native American spirituality, or are an agnostic or atheist. Whatever their personal beliefs, the Steps challenge PIRs to accept that they are not the center of the universe, and to find a power greater than themselves, a "Higher Power"—something or someone they can turn to for guidance and support. A Higher Power can be defined however one chooses to define it. Some might call their Higher Power God; others might define it as nature, the positive energy of their group, or an unnamed sense of spirit.

PIRs talk about "working the Steps" because they return to them again and again as they deal with ongoing life challenges and changes. The Twelve Steps are so practical that they can serve as a philosophical guide for anyone— whether or not they belong to a Twelve Step group. They are useful tools to measure, chart, and stimulate inner growth.

The Twelve Steps are often summed up succinctly as follows: problem, solution, and plan of action. Step One defines the problem (powerlessness over addiction), Steps Two and Three point to a solution (a Higher Power), and the remaining Steps lay out the plan for living a saner and more fulfilling life. When I read the Steps for the first time, I was struck by the fact that all that is really asked of people is a *willingness* to change.

Here are the Twelve Steps of Alcoholics Anonymous:[13]

STEP ONE: *We admitted we were powerless over alcohol—that our lives had become unmanageable.* (The NA text reads "We admitted we were powerless over our addiction, that our lives had become unmanageable.") This of course is a huge step, as so many PIRs prior to recovery were in great denial that they could ever be an addict. For alcoholics and addicts, Step One means admitting they finally realize that once they start using alcohol or other drugs, they can't stop.

STEP TWO: *Came to believe that a Power greater than ourselves could restore us to sanity.* It is important for addicts to believe in some power outside themselves, since they have just admitted that they lack the power to stop drinking or using on their own.

STEP THREE: *Made a decision to turn our will and our lives over to the care of God* as we understood Him. The end of this sentence is very important, for many reasons. Even back in the day when the Big Book was written, Bill W. and others knew that many addicts run away from religious concepts, and Bill W. and the early creators of AA did not want anyone to be turned off, thinking they were being told they needed to believe a certain way. Bill W. struggled with this himself until a friend asked, "Why don't you choose your own conception of God?" Times have changed since then, but the idea is still the same: everyone who follows the Twelve Steps is encouraged to shape their own idea of a Higher Power into whatever is most meaningful and useful for them.

Steps Four through Ten are sometimes called the "relationship" Steps, and they'll be discussed in more detail in the next chapter. But here's a brief description of each of them:

STEP FOUR: *Made a searching and fearless moral inventory of ourselves.* In this Step, PIRs look deeply within themselves and list their character traits, behaviors (harm they have caused when using), and addictive thoughts and feelings that feed addictive behavior and get in the way of recovery. They also acknowledge their character strengths that can help them stay clean and sober.

STEP FIVE: *Admitted to God, to ourselves, and to another human being the exact nature of our wrongs.* As powerful as it may be for PIRs to admit their character flaws to themselves, honestly sharing these flaws with another human being and with their Higher Power is a huge step that can bring their true self into even sharper focus.

STEP SIX: *Were entirely ready to have God remove all these defects of character.* This sounds easier than it actually is because many PIRs have grown so used to their addictive thinking and behaviors that it can be tough to let them go. But all that's required in Step Six is a willingness to move in a spiritual direction.

STEP SEVEN: *Humbly asked Him to remove our shortcomings.* The "Him" refers to whatever PIRs have named as their Higher Power, and in this Step they ask that source beyond themselves for guidance in letting go of their roadblocks to recovery.

STEP EIGHT: *Made a list of all persons we had harmed, and became willing to make amends to them all.* Addiction is like a bulldozer that can run over many who get in its path. Listing those they've harmed—whether living or dead—helps PIRs get over the denial they may still cling to that their drinking or drugging only hurt themselves.

STEP NINE: *Made direct amends to such people wherever possible, except when to do so would injure them or others.* Many PIRs tell me that this is the most difficult Step of all because they come face-to-face with the harm their addictive behavior has caused others and, in doing so, they take responsibility for their actions.

STEP TEN: *Continued to take personal inventory and when we were wrong promptly admitted it.* This is what "working a program" is all about. None of us—perhaps especially those in recovery—can guarantee we will never make another mistake or harm another person. Step Ten is a reminder of the importance of daily check-ins and the need to "nip problems in the bud" so they don't turn into crises.

STEP ELEVEN: *Sought through prayer and meditation to improve our conscious contact with God* as we understood Him, *praying only for knowledge of His will for us and the power to carry that out.* This Step is a reminder of how important it is for PIRs to stay spiritually centered and remember to "get out of their own way" by trusting in a power greater than and beyond themselves.

STEP TWELVE: *Having had a spiritual awakening as the result of these steps, we tried to carry this message to alcoholics, and to practice these principles in all our affairs.* The Big Book stresses the importance of PIRs getting involved in something greater than themselves, of helping out however they are able. They will often go to locations in which people need to hear about AA and what it can do for them. My newly recovering PIR was thrilled because he'd been asked to speak at our local prison.

PIRs who are serious about working their program study these Steps intensely and put them into action, often with the aid of AA books like *Twelve Steps and Twelve Traditions, Living Sober,* and *Came to Believe.* Many PIRs also do the Steps by using one of the many workbooks available online or that they may have gotten from a counselor when they were in treatment. Of course, AA and NA members also use the Big Book and the NA basic text mentioned in chapter 1. In a recent meeting that I attended, someone spoke very highly of *Living Sober,* describing it as a practical and basic guidebook for his sobriety. He said that the Big Book was more "like Shakespeare" to him because it was written in an old-fashioned style that hearkens back to the 1930s, when AA was founded. But he said he loved reading the Big Book stories of how the first members became sober and the stories that were added in later editions. "Reading all those stories of so many different people in long-term recovery gives me hope that I can do it too," he told me.

I feel that everyone, PIRs and non-PIRs, can benefit
from following the Twelve Steps in their lives. I personally
became better acquainted with the Twelve Steps when I
began attending Al-Anon meetings. Al-Anon is the worldwide organization devoted to the spouses, significant others, and families of alcoholics. There is a similar group,
called Nar-Anon, that focuses on the spouses, families, and
significant others of people who are addicted to drugs. In
the same manner that AA and NA help PIRs, these two organizations have helped countless others who are in relationships with PIRs. They both utilize the Twelve Steps, and
they both use the Twelve Traditions as their organizational
guidelines for anonymity and core principles.

I have to admit that I barely knew anything about Al-
Anon when Steve and I began our relationship. For some
reason, no one ever suggested that I attend an Al-Anon
meeting, even though I was dating someone who was fairly
new to the recovery program. I think, looking back, that I
was still in the mind-set of "look, he's not drinking, so things
must be normal now." At any rate, I didn't start attending
Al-Anon until about a month after Steve and I broke up.
(It actually was more like a "fizzle-out," as he just stopped
calling me.) I was pretty much a mess, smarting from the
breakup, wondering what in the heck had gone on in my life
during the time we were together. Seeing how upset and be-
wildered I was, a PIR friend urged me to attend an Al-Anon
meeting.

So I looked up Al-Anon online, and found a local early
evening meeting in an office building not far from where I
live. I walked into the fairly small room, which had chairs
lining the walls and a table in the middle where the person

who led the meeting sat. People gradually began filling these chairs and introducing themselves to me before the meeting started. I listened to the stories of others who, like me, were (or had been) in a relationship with a PIR. In less than five minutes, I was a crying mess, and I continued crying on and off throughout the whole meeting. Someone offered me a box of Kleenex, and I kept it very close. Everyone was really sympathetic and told me afterward that they'd done the same thing at their first meeting. I felt such a relief, knowing that others understood my mixture of emotions, my confusion, and my pain. It's probably the same type of relief PIRs feel when they first walk into an NA or AA meeting. I experienced such a sense of love and empathy. I felt a tremendous amount of strength and spirituality in that room. Some of these people were dealing with lifelong issues with their parents, kids, or spouses. Many of their "qualifiers," as they called their loved ones, were still drinking or using, not sober like my PIR was.

Al-Anon meetings are structured similarly to the AA meetings described above. We had a leader, who led us in reciting the Serenity Prayer. I had read the words before, but their meaning was entirely different when I applied them to myself and to my situation. *"God, grant me the serenity to accept the things I cannot change, courage to change the things I can, and wisdom to know the difference."* Even at that first meeting, I was starting to see how I had no more control over my PIR or his recovery than he had over his addiction to alcohol.

There were introductions, followed by the leader briefly talking about organizational business. She then told us the "theme" for the night, and we read passages from a little book called *Courage to Change*. Then there was a discussion of the readings, and those who wished to could take a turn and explain how the theme related to them. Finally, we closed with the Lord's Prayer, and then adjourned to the next room for coffee.

In Al-Anon, I came to find out that the very nature of this disease called addiction is "focus-draining." My PIR was in recovery, and he had to make that his top priority, for his own survival. Without even realizing it, I fell into an unhealthy pattern of also focusing on him and his addiction and recovery, losing myself in the process. Al-Anon helped me put the focus back on *me* and helped me take care of my own self.

I stayed in Al-Anon until I was able to put together the pieces of what had happened in my relationship with Steve and felt strong enough to give the experience distance. But I continue to practice what I learned in Al-Anon, and will be so much smarter about everything if and when I enter into another relationship with a PIR. And I know the door to Al-Anon is always open if I need that kind of support again. If you haven't already tried it, especially if you're already in a relationship with a PIR, I urge you to give Al-Anon or Nar-Anon a try. How I wish I'd had that knowledge and Al-Anon tools and support when I was dating Steve! I also attend a wonderful church that helped me so much during my relationship and after my breakup, and I continue to be so grateful for the support and spiritual guidance I get there.

I mentioned how the Serenity Prayer has a different (and deeper) meaning now that I apply it to me and to my own life, and not just think of it as something my PIR recited at his AA meetings. The same is true of the Twelve

Steps. In Al-Anon, I learned that every one of the Steps can be applied to someone who is in a relationship with a PIR. We who care about a PIR are also powerless over alcohol and other drugs and—try as we might—we can't control whether or not the PIR uses them. We who are often affected by the craziness that addictive behavior can cause can also have our sanity restored by trusting in a Higher Power for guidance. And we can also become healthier in body, mind, and spirit if we honestly acknowledge our faults, celebrate our strengths, and become accountable on a daily basis for our actions and reactions—especially the ones that have harmed others.

In the next chapter we'll look at how Steps Four through Ten (the "relationship" Steps) pertain to both PIRs and their partners.

[4]

Why Some People Call Steps Four through Ten the "Relationship" Steps

MENDING RELATIONSHIPS that were broken due to addiction is an ongoing task in recovery. Many PIRs also need help establishing healthy relationships. Some PIRs come from unhappy families in which emotional or physical abuse and addiction were common. Because of this, some PIRs may have developed trust, intimacy, or abandonment issues. As a result, they might view dysfunctional relationships as normal and seek out these types of unhealthy relationships in their new sober life, unless they are made aware of what they are doing and work diligently to release and heal their past. When they were drinking and using, they may have grown used to doing whatever it took to cover up, excuse, or engage in their addictive behavior. When it comes to an addiction disorder, deceit, manipulation, and friendships with fellow drinking or drugging buddies are too often the rule, rather than the exception. In other words, there's often a lot for them to "unlearn" in recovery.

In Twelve Step programs, and especially in Steps Four through Ten, PIRs learn how to develop healthy relationship skills. They work on taking responsibility for the harm they have caused others, and acknowledge the harm that others have caused them. Ultimately, these Steps are about asking for forgiveness and forgiving others. In these Steps, PIRs practice reaching out to other people and face their fear of rejection. In the process, they learn mutual respect for others and how to have equality in a relationship rather than power over someone else.

When I mentioned to my friend Mark that I was writing this chapter, he said, "Yikes! That's enough for a whole book!" He then proceeded to tell me about his own struggles and achievements as he worked on each of these "relationship" Steps. Sometimes these Steps take a long time to work through the first time, and because recovery and relationships are ongoing realities, these are Steps that are revisited time and time again.

You may meet your PIR while they are in the midst of working Steps Four through Ten and be curious about what this "amends making" is all about. I was so unfamiliar with the Twelve Steps that I didn't know enough to ask Steve about them or if he had done them. And I certainly didn't know that, as someone in a relationship with a PIR, it would have been good for me to do these Steps as well. Now I've discovered that these "relationship" Steps are a balanced, healthy way even for non-PIRs to examine their own selves and their relationships with others. But the Steps are especially useful if you *are* dating a PIR, because the skills you learn from the Steps may be helpful in your relationship.

Step Four asks people to make "a searching and fearless moral inventory" of themselves. As the Big Book explains it, a personal inventory works much like a business inventory, similar to when a store owner sorts through his or her goods to see which are salable, which are damaged, and which have to be thrown out. When PIRs do a personal inventory, they list the things—their thoughts, feelings, character traits, and behaviors—that stand in the way of recovery and those personal strengths that can help in recovery. A business that tries to sell useless or damaged things goes broke; a PIR who holds on to useless and unhealthy thoughts, feelings, and behaviors also goes "broke" and risks relapse.

The Big Book, page 64, says that "resentment is the 'number one' offender," and that it destroys more addicts than anything else does. It is obviously very important, therefore, for PIRs to identify and release their resentments in a constructive way. My friend Paul told me about helping PIRs make "resentment lists." He said at first they'll say "heck no, I don't have any resentments," until they actually start listing the people and things that make them angry. Paul said that the more thorough the list, the better, in order to make sure the PIR deals with any smoldering resentments (or other thoughts and feelings) that might creep out later in an unhealthy way.

The moral inventory in Step Four gives PIRs a practical tool for honestly and courageously facing how their addictive actions may have hurt others and harmed themselves in the process. There is no right or wrong way to do this Step, and those who work it don't stop to try to figure out why they did what they did—they merely make a list in whatever way works best for them, trying to be as "searching and fearless" as they can be. After listing their resentments, many PIRs include in their lists the other categories suggested in the Big Book:

- fears
- people we have harmed
- sexual harms done to others

This last category of sexual harms is not limited to actual physical harms like infecting someone with a sexually transmitted disease, or having sex with someone against their will. This category also gets the PIR thinking about how they were inconsiderate with their partner, how they might have been jealous or suspicious, or how they might have cheated on their partner. Paul told me that, for him, the easiest part was to remember and list all the people he had harmed. It was harder for him to admit the sexual harms he'd done and the people he'd used when he was still drinking. But he said he needed to face those things if he ever hoped to have a healthy relationship—sexual and otherwise—in the future.

When people work Step Four, they begin to realize that in order to stay clean and sober, they need to handle all their feelings—the good, the bad, and the ugly ones—in a healthy and safe way rather than covering them up with mood-altering chemicals or addictive behaviors. Many PIRs who have numbed their feelings for so long start to actually feel again. Others might become ready to face past traumas such as sexual, physical, or emotional abuse, and they might realize they need professional help to deal with painful and upsetting memories. If you sense (or know) this is the case with your PIR, it's good to give them some space and lots of tender support and encouragement, remembering that you can't be their therapist, but you can be their friend.

The soul searching and the fearlessness with which PIRs work on Step Four can make for a deeper and more meaningful relationship with their partners. What an amazing step for anyone to take. What a help it can be to know that your PIR has had the guts to look inside and come up with so many things they want to change and improve.

When I tried out Step Four for myself, I discovered just how difficult it is to take an honest look within oneself. It's much easier to use our PIR and his or her addiction as a convenient scapegoat for all *our* troubles—especially our relationship troubles. Working Step Four for ourselves can bring to the surface our own lingering fears, feelings of bitterness, impatience, or despair. In looking at our own assets and liabilities, we sort out the qualities that can help in our relationship and we learn to own our stuff—those thoughts, feelings, and behaviors that can stand in the way of honestly connecting with someone else. When we take responsibility for our own behavior—listing those people we've harmed and acknowledging the less-than-wonderful things we've done—we realize no one is perfect, which makes it a little easier to accept our PIR and their past.

As challenging as it can be, Step Four is an exercise in humility that sets the stage for Step Five: *Admitted to God, to ourselves, and to another human being the exact nature of our wrongs.* The authors of the Big Book were adamant about completing Step Five, emphasizing how necessary it is for recovery.

Paul and his wife Sandy, who is also a PIR, say that Step Five can be difficult because a PIR has to actually admit to someone else—out loud—what they've done in the past and who they've harmed. They tell other PIRs that they might want to share their Fourth Step inventory with their sponsor, or with a priest, rabbi, or trusted friend who is familiar with the Twelve Steps and who can listen to their inventory without interrupting or judging them. Because it's essential that people who work the Fourth Step be as honest as possible, I don't think it's a good idea to have (or expect) your PIR to share his or her inventory with you—or for you to share yours with your PIR if you're in a Twelve Step program such as Al-Anon or Nar-Anon. It's natural to want to protect a partner or to censor some of the things you think might disturb them. A Step Four inventory can be a lot to absorb all at once!

Paul remarked that there is sometimes an ironic aspect to sharing an inventory. He said it can be a tremendous relief to discover that the horrible things you've had a hard time admitting sometimes don't seem so horrible to someone else. "All your life you've felt such shame and guilt about something you've done, and then you admit it to the other person, and they say, 'So what was so bad about that?' When you review your faults and your strengths with someone, you usually find you aren't as awful—or as wonderful!—as you might think!"

Paul said that when a PIR admits to someone else the issues they may have held inside for many years, they have taken a huge step on both an individual level and a relationship level. The fact that your PIR is learning to be more open and is able to talk to someone about what are often very intimate issues can be an exceptionally positive thing in a relationship. Being candid with others will, no doubt, help them be more honest with you about feelings and issues that might arise. This also gives you permission to be honest and open with your PIR.

My friend Seth said he learned so much from this Step.

He and his wife Pam now have an emotionally solid marriage in which they can feel free to discuss anything that bothers them in a loving and noncritical way. He credits this, in large part, to having worked Steps Four and Five—Steps they both put to good use by practicing Step Ten, where you incorporate Steps Four through Nine into your daily life. He said neither of them came into the marriage with the communication skills they now have after many years together, and he admits it took a lot of work and patience to get to where they're at now. He said doing Steps Four and Five when he first began his recovery program gave him an important foundation on which to build his marriage.

Steps Four and Five are major recovery—and relationship—milestones that can leave our PIRs (and us, if we're working the Twelve Steps of Al-Anon or Nar-Anon) emotionally and physically exhausted. This is why the Big Book suggests taking some quiet time to reflect on the experience. Accepting our faults and celebrating our strengths is hard work!

The NA basic text talks about how Step Six—*Were entirely ready to have God remove all these defects of character*—is about moving in a spiritual direction, from self toward something beyond self. Paul and Sandy said that, for them, this Step was a relief after all the work they did on Steps Four and Five. But for some other PIRs, it can be very difficult to let go of their addictive habits and thoughts, some of which they may have had for a very long time. If they are still clinging to something they can't let go of, they continue to ask their Higher Power to help them release it. Some PIRs might turn to their recovery group for advice, others might practice meditation, and still others might seek guidance through prayer to a God of their understanding. The goal is to be *willing* to let these things go, so that they can move forward on their spiritual path.

This willingness is also a positive factor in a healthy relationship with a PIR. Give-and-take in a relationship is important. Sandy said that willingness is probably her most positive trait, one that she learned and keeps practicing in recovery. She said she used to be very stubborn and confessed she still can be, at times. She admitted she sometimes still resists Paul's suggestions at first, but will come to a middle ground with him much more easily these days, after working (and reworking) Step Six. Paul laughingly called Sandy's process "willingness with resistance," but he acknowledged that he, too, can see what a difference being *willing* to change has made for each of them—and for their relationship—as they both continue to work their recovery.

Identifying one's shortcomings, then working to remove them, is an important ongoing exercise for both PIRs *and* their partners. There are many personal characteristics that get in the way of building a healthy, balanced relationship that are not just aspects of addiction. For instance, how many of us struggle with things like lack of acceptance, or, unlike Sandy, how many of us often feel unwilling to open ourselves to change? How many of us have control issues or fall prey to irrational fear, selfishness, jealousy, or dishonesty? What about anger or resentment or dishonesty or self-pity?

Step Seven is about acknowledging these traits—our "shortcomings"—and *humbly* handing them over to a power greater than ourselves. PIRs might ask their Higher Power to remove some addictive traits that they are stubbornly hanging on to. The rest of us might want to get rid of some other character defects, such as the ones mentioned above.

I especially like the use of the word "humbly" in this Step. PIRs are learning to deal with their addict-centered egos; they are realizing that they are not the center of the universe. They are learning that there is something greater than themselves, and are beginning to trust this Higher Power. Above all, they are learning to relinquish the control tactics that developed because of addiction. They are humbly asking, rather than selfishly demanding, that their Higher Power help them. This very likely is the type of mind-set you'd wish for in your dating partner *and* in yourself.

"Let go and let God" is a popular phrase in recovery groups. Your PIR is learning to do exactly this, and we can all benefit from doing the same—releasing our need to direct and control everything, and handing over our undesirable traits. When we rid ourselves of unwanted and troublesome character defects, we make room in our relationships for the qualities we want—qualities like love, honesty, courage, compassion, unselfishness, and acceptance.

Step Eight—*Made a list of all persons we had harmed, and became willing to make amends to them all*—can sometimes be the most difficult Step for the PIR. In the same humble way that they approached their Higher Power in Step Seven, they must look past their own egos and their patterns of addictive denial to recognize those whom they have hurt. Their list can contain both people who are living and those who have died. They make sure to leave no one off the list, no matter how hard they think it will be to make amends to that person. Often the list includes family members with whom they have had many years of dysfunction. It may include you, if you were in a relationship with your PIR before they began working a recovery program. If the PIR has thoroughly worked their previous Steps and released their resentments or anger, this Step will be smoother for them, and they can then become more willing to make their amends.

Many PIRs have told me that becoming aware of those they have harmed was a huge step for them. They said this awareness is especially important in new relationships because it helps them not to repeat old patterns. Those of you who are dating a PIR will also become aware of your past patterns in relationships if you follow this Step, and you can then integrate your knowledge into your new relationship with your PIR.

We might think that it makes perfect sense for our PIR to list everyone who has been injured by addictive behavior and be willing to make amends to them, but it has little to do with us. Or it might be difficult for us to get beyond how our PIR's addiction has harmed us—especially those of us who have been in a long-term relationship with a PIR. But what about our obsession with the problem? What has that done to others? Have we been so preoccupied with our PIR and his or her addictive behavior that we've neglected others? Acknowledging that we, too, may have harmed others frees us to conduct our relationships—all of our relationships—in an honest, loving, and healthy way.

All Step Eight asks for is honesty and willingness to make amends. Those who work this Step are advised to do so without worrying too much about actually making amends yet. The thinking is that this kind of worry might prevent them from being honest about listing all of the people they've harmed.

My friend Paul calls Step Nine—*Made direct amends to such people wherever possible, except when to do so would injure them or others*—"the killer Step." It took my friend Mark two years to complete this the first time he worked the Twelve Steps. Some PIRs never complete it, and they risk continued relationship dysfunction and possible relapse as a result. In Step Nine, PIRs face up to the damage their addictive behaviors have caused, and take responsibility for their own actions. In doing this Step, they are actually facing the people whom they have hurt and asking their forgiveness.

In the Big Book, there is a section on how to do this Step. Some PIRs who are new to recovery, the section mentions, may have an almost too-good-to-believe new persona that their families and friends may distrust. PIRs making their amends are thus cautioned not to sound too "religious" or overbearing, nor to sound critical or argumentative. To help the PIR approach someone they want to make amends with, the Big Book says: "We go to him in a helpful and forgiving spirit, confessing our former ill feeling and expressing our regret. . . . In nine cases out of ten the unexpected happens. Sometimes the man we are calling upon admits his own fault, so feuds of years' standing melt away in an hour."[14]

PIRs are also counseled not to get upset if the person to whom they have made amends is not willing to forgive them. The Ninth Step is important for their own growth, their own recovery, and their own future relationships. They are told "It should not matter, however, if someone does throw us out of his office. We have made our demonstration, done our part. It's water over the dam."[15] Put another way, making amends is about how the person making them acts—not how the other person reacts. If your PIR has you on his or her list and makes amends to you for past hurts, you need to be honest about how you feel. You may not be able to forgive and forget right away, and this may be a critical time for deciding if this relationship can work. Just as your PIR is doing this to stay sober, you will need to work through and honestly share your own feelings to take care of yourself, not out of fear of upsetting your PIR. When both of you are honest, you will have a better chance of putting the past behind you and eventually finding real forgiveness for a more trusting and open relationship.

The latter part of the Step, *except when to do so would injure them or others,* is something the PIR has to consider very seriously. What if the PIR, for example, is the sole breadwinner in the family, and by coming clean with their issue, they also end up going to jail, thus depriving the family of income? There can be some big moral dilemmas in which making amends is not the wisest thing to do at that time. PIRs are counseled to do the right thing, so as not to place undue harm on the people they have already hurt by their addiction.

My friends Sandy and Paul were very helpful in explaining to me their views on Step Nine. Sandy said, "The amends are for *you,* not the other person. You get the amends out, then step away." She said that her Ninth Step wasn't too hard for her and that she felt a huge relief after completing it. She also said it helped to put her old relationship patterns into perspective. Paul said he was glad he did his Ninth Step because he knows how *not* doing it can adversely affect all of a person's relationships.

I've learned from my friends and from Al-Anon how important it is to make amends to people when I've hurt them, and how the process of making amends teaches us about forgiveness. Forgiving others and being forgiven lessens the guilt and resentment we might carry. I've also learned that it's not enough to just say "I'm sorry," and that making amends should match the harm that was caused. For example, if a PIR makes amends for stealing money from a friend but makes no move to pay the money back, the amends are somewhat meaningless. Empty "I'm sorries" in a relationship work the same way.

Paul and Sandy are a good example of a successful relationship that has endured, in part because they both did thorough work on their Steps. They met in recovery. Each was dating someone else at the time. Sandy had been sober twelve years; Paul for one year. They've known each other for eighteen years and have been married for five and a half years. (I was at their wedding!) They describe their relationship as being based on "complete freedom and openness," by "practicing honesty in all ways." As Sandy re-emphasized, she feels her most positive trait is willingness, which she developed in recovery. Paul says his most positive trait is that he doesn't take things so seriously anymore—he lets things roll off him. He has more patience, generally—another thing he learned in recovery. "Except with her!" he added jokingly. Lightheartedness is something else they say that recovery has given them. They each have a great sense of humor, and neither one hesitates to take a little loving jab at the other one, which to me is endearing and fun and seems to keep their relationship alive.

My friend Mark agrees that Step Nine was especially challenging. Besides making amends to those he'd harmed, he also had a lot of work to do in forgiving his parents for all the dysfunction in his childhood. His mother was mentally unstable and abusive, and his dad left the family when Mark was young. Mark was the eldest of five boys, and it fell upon him to help take care of his brothers. He also had bouts of depression starting at age eight, and began drinking at age eleven. His mom died when he was seventeen years old and she was just thirty-six. They had had a fight in the hospital right before she died. So his Ninth Step was very important to him and took a while to do. He obviously could not make direct amends to his mother, so he had to handle his amends to her with the help of meditation. He said that after he finished his Ninth Step, he felt wonderfully light and ready to do the rest of the Steps. His emotions were clearer to him, and he looked forward to healthier relationships. His former girlfriend, Barb, recalled the talk they'd had when he was making amends to her, in which he sounded clearer than she'd heard him be in years. It was a very positive experience for both of them.

Step Ten—*Continued to take personal inventory and when we were wrong promptly admitted it*—is a reminder that recovery is an ongoing process. PIRs who truly "work their recovery program" are always working on themselves, always monitoring their day-by-day actions and reactions to make sure their addictive behaviors and practices are kept at bay. If one of these behaviors pops up, they take the steps to fix it so situations don't get worse. PIRs can never guarantee that they won't hurt someone again, nor make mistakes along the way, but they now have tools to help them. Almost every PIR I talked to for this book acknowledged how much this Step helps them. They say it's a reminder that they are human and, of course, will make mistakes, just like non-PIRs. Taking a personal inventory, one day at a time, is a healthy and balanced way to live—for both a PIR and his or her partner.

The second part of the Step, *and when we were wrong promptly admitted it,* is challenging, but it is something a PIR who has worked Steps Four through Nine now has the tools to do. This is an important skill for anyone in any type of relationship, but it's an especially handy one for a PIR in a dating relationship. We can all benefit from "getting over ourselves" and admitting when we're wrong. How much easier it is to have a partner who has already worked on this, and how important it is for us to practice this skill ourselves!

Paul and Sandy found that they can easily get through any relationship challenges because they both work their programs. They admit their own mistakes right away, discuss things honestly, and move on. The same is true for Pam and Seth. Pam says that the two of them "talk, talk, talk," and Seth told me that within fifteen minutes of an argument, they move on to trying to get everything out in the open and discussing it. Each of them has learned how to be more flexible so they can see the other's point of view. Seth said he's learned from the Twelve Step program (and from years of therapy) how to "be real and not cover up" issues he had to contend with in his past. Pam says that, for her, it was a process of learning how to balance things. They are now very mindful of each other, and "check in" with each other daily.

As you can see from reading about those who have worked Steps Four through Ten, the process is challenging, rewarding, and continuous. After working the "relationship" Steps, PIRs know themselves better and have the tools to continue to self-monitor. The outcome is a life with richer, more fulfilling, and honest relationships.

[5]

Addictive Behaviors Don't Magically Disappear

ABOUT ONE MONTH into my relationship with Steve, I began to question some of his quirks and behaviors. He was starting to cancel some of our dates, or, if he did show up, he would be extremely late and offer some lame excuse. He was threatening to quit a brand-new job with no clear reason, which just didn't make sense to me. I began to wonder if these things were typical of PIRs. I've since learned that addictive thinking, like addictive behavior, is something that PIRs continually deal with throughout their recovery.

Addictive thinking is a distorted way of thinking that is associated with addiction disorders, and one of the main aspects of addictive thinking is denial. Addicts use denial as a way of warping reality to the point where they actually believe that what they are saying is the truth, even when it defies all evidence to the contrary. In the midst of addiction, alcoholics and drug addicts in denial might convince themselves they can drink and use like anybody else or quit anytime they want to. They might deny they have a problem because they're ashamed or cannot accept the fact that they are not in control. The main reason for their denial, though, is to protect their desperate need to feed their addiction at all costs. One woman I read about drank nearly a bottle of vodka every day, yet denied she had a problem, saying, "Me? I'm not an alcoholic! I have a prestigious job, an expensive house, and several college degrees! I am not like the people on the street who want handouts." My friend Tim used to say, "Hey, if I can get up and go to work on Monday, I don't have a problem."

Unfortunately, denial is something that can creep back into a PIR's life during their recovery. After a period of successful abstinence, they might be convinced that they can control their use or, if their problem was alcohol, they might think, "A joint now and then can't hurt anything." Sometimes this addictive thinking is "contagious," leading those who date PIRs to think the same way: "He seems to have his drinking under control, so one beer can't hurt anything." "Her drug of choice was cocaine, so we can still enjoy a cocktail now and then."

This type of rationalization reinforces a PIR's denial because their explanations and excuses for their behavior often make sense on the surface. Rationalization can also preserve the status quo for alcoholics and addicts because it gives them an excuse not to change anything about their situation. Change is tough for all of us, but it can be especially hard for an addict. How much easier it is for all of us to offer a good explanation (or lame excuse), and continue doing what we've been doing. So it makes sense that this tendency to rationalize and resist change doesn't just disappear for PIRs after they've quit using. This is why the Serenity Prayer is usually recited in recovery meetings: *God, grant me the serenity to accept the things I cannot change, courage to change the things I can, and wisdom to know the difference.* It's a statement of surrender and letting go, and a reminder for PIRs *and* those in a relationship with them that no one can control everything, that everyone has choices, and that we all need support and guidance from a Higher Power—a source of strength beyond ourselves—to help us make healthy decisions and act wisely.

Blaming others for one's own behavior can also reinforce denial and continue the status quo. From what PIRs have told me, blaming someone else relieved them from taking responsibility for making changes when they were using. In recovery, PIRs learn that they cannot change anyone but themselves, so throughout recovery they practice being responsible by working on their tendencies to deny, rationalize, and blame.

I wish I'd known this sooner. When I hung out with my PIR and his friends, they would sometimes get in a conversational loop in which they would blame their ex-wives or ex-girlfriends for just about everything that was going wrong. This bugged me to no end, and I didn't realize why until I found out how blaming and addiction are related. Granted, we all tend to blame others at times, but knowing the big role that blaming plays in addiction helped me better understand PIRs. Besides, as I pointed out in chapter 2, many PIRs came from homes where shaming and blaming were the norm, so it's even tougher for them to "unlearn" these behaviors.

Manipulation is another form of addictive thinking and behavior that I consider serious and even scary. When I first learned about it, I thought, "Who in their right mind would put up with something like this?" Then it occurred to me—I did, and so did my friend Grace (see below). When they are in the midst of addiction, many addicts often use people to get what they want. They may convince a friend to go and buy them booze or get them some cocaine. They may beg a relative for money, making the excuse that they need it for food or for rent.

I asked my PIR friends if they did this when they were using, and they admitted they sure did. My friend Greg said that back in his using days he dated a girl he described as a "borderline addict." He said he would manipulate her into using drugs with him by first getting her drunk on several bottles of wine. Then, when her defenses were down, he'd convince her to do cocaine with him. She came from a wealthy family, and he admits thinking that if he could get her hooked on drugs like he was, she could supply the drug money for both of them.

Manipulation also means being talked into something you don't want to do. For example, my PIR convinced me to loan him a significant amount of money. Twice. My friend Grace was convinced by her PIR husband, Joe, that they had to move back and forth between several different states during the ten years of their marriage. She later found out it was because Joe was trying to get out of paying years of child support he owed. She said, "He was a pretty good salesman to convince me to move all those times." Joe had been in recovery for years by this point, yet he was still practicing addictive behavior. (Joe has since passed away.) Of course, Grace and I could have said "no" to our PIRs, but at that time we didn't understand manipulative behavior—or enabling, which will be covered in an upcoming chapter.

I learned from talking to my friends in recovery that

they share several deep-seated ways of thinking and behaving that many of them trace to their childhood. Learning about these behavioral traits and how they relate to addiction helped me better understand my boyfriend.

For example, lots of these friends continue to work on low self-esteem. While many of us may also feel "less than" from time to time, addicts often come to believe in this reality, and will subsequently use alcohol or other drugs to self-medicate as a means of escaping painful feelings. Apparently, PIRs aren't always aware of how low their self-esteem is when they first enter recovery. I read a story of a PIR who went to a doctor for treatment after being fired from her job due to her alcoholism. He asked her to list some redeeming qualities about herself, and she couldn't think of anything. He reminded her that she had graduated from college *magna cum laude* and had been inducted into Phi Beta Kappa—one of the most prestigious honor societies in the country. She told him that when she'd been told she was chosen for this honor, she was sure they'd made a mistake.

I discovered that trying to boost a PIR's self-esteem can be hard work, and trying to convince someone that they matter in the here and now, and did matter prior to the addiction, requires much time and patience. This is where recovery comes in. In recovery, PIRs are taught through positive reinforcement that they do, indeed, have the coping skills they never thought they had. They also learn that they have a disease, and they are not at fault for having this disease. These revelations and the other work they do in recovery can greatly improve their self-image.

Almost everyone I interviewed, both those who had

dated PIRs and PIRs themselves, found low self-esteem to be a prevalent factor in addiction and in recovery. Ed had incredibly low self-esteem that he attributed to a harsh and demanding father who did not allow him to make mistakes. Ed worked very hard in high school and college to assure himself of a good career, and he learned to cover up his feelings. Craving approval, he became a people-pleaser who was terrified of rejection. When old feelings of inadequacy would surface, he quelled them with alcohol. He landed in AA after two painful events: getting a divorce and getting fired from his job. Following these events, he was "rudderless" for five years until, eventually, he learned to accept help. First, he began the practice of daily prayer; second, he began to open up more and to share his feelings with others in recovery, asking them how they solved their self-esteem issues. It took him at least another three years, but he finally became accepting of himself.

My friend Seth said he's always had problems with low self-esteem. He started drinking and using at age seventeen, and didn't admit he had a problem until he was thirty-five years old. His friends had strongly suggested that he had a problem, but he was in denial about it for several years. He said he'd drink and use pot at the same time, which resulted in "awful trips." He said he began isolating himself more and more, and when he did venture out, he "went incognito." One night in a bar, he hit bottom. He blacked out, and was literally thrown out of the bar onto the street outside, still in his suit from work. His front teeth were broken in the process. He was "in a stupor" for five days, and then he went into his place of work and shared what happened with his boss. His boss, ironically, had just started recovery himself, and was very sympathetic. In fact, it was his boss who finally convinced Seth to join AA.

Seth has been in therapy for most of his sober adulthood, but says he continues to work on his low self-esteem. A creative, sensitive child, he grew up in a family where he felt like he didn't belong. His father did not understand Seth's artistic side and came down hard on him for not being "manly" enough. Seth didn't find out that he was adopted until he was a young adult, and he felt betrayed by his family when they finally told him this truth. He later found out that his biological mother was an alcoholic. He told me that he entered adulthood feeling a sense of rejection, of not measuring up. He also said he realized he had suppressed anger, at women in particular. This became quite an issue when he began dating Pam, a non-PIR, who is now his wife. They met at a spiritual retreat when Seth had been sober for fifteen months. Their first date was an open AA meeting, but Seth said he wasn't "spiritually evolved" yet and wasn't ready for a serious commitment. So he continued to date other people, eventually moving out of state to continue to work on his recovery. Pam, though, wrote him often, and Seth joked, "She seduced me with her letters." She moved so that she could be with him, and they were soon married. Thanks to the hard work they've both done in Seth's recovery, their marriage is solid, and Seth's self-image continues to improve.

PIRs are often described as having "big egos with an inferiority complex inside." Ironically, sometimes PIRs try to make up for low self-esteem by going to the other extreme—which is called "grandiosity" in recovery groups. Either trait—grandiosity or low self-esteem—can present challenges if you are dating a PIR. In a romantic relationship, both lack of self-esteem and an inflated ego can manifest in an obsessive demand for affection from one's partner. In the early stages of recovery, some PIRs can be very needy, which is one reason dating a PIR in the first year or so of recovery is frowned upon. As my PIR friend Mark explains, most PIRs are too preoccupied with working their Steps and putting their lives back together to have a relationship in the first year or two of recovery.

Many PIRs often think and act in extremes, showing little flexibility or consideration for alternatives. Many also tend toward the extremes in their feelings or ambitions. This "either-or" thinking often results in PIRs exaggerating their problems, overgeneralizing (reaching a general conclusion based on a single experience), and jumping to conclusions.

I'm thinking again of my friend Grace and her husband Joe. Seeing no middle ground in his child-support issues, he would tell her, "I'm going with or without you." Then off he would move once again, and Grace would go along. I'm happy to report that they eventually settled down in a stable location and he finally began to work on his debts.

My boyfriend Steve was one of those PIRs who liked to go to extremes in his leisure time. He had to drive his car fast; he had to have a booming sound system in it. He "went at it" in very high gear. I learned that behaviors like this can be something of a substitute for using. Some PIRs describe themselves as still needing a high level of excitement or pleasure. They say they are bored if they are not always involved in a thrilling, and sometimes risky, activity. My PIR liked to drive fast so much that he eventually joined a motocross club that met in the next county. This was actually very good exercise and fun for him, and I would go watch him race.

In the introduction to this book, I confessed that I am often attracted to people who have issues that mirror my own. Like so many PIRs I know and have dated, I also suffer from low self-esteem, and I am the epitome of an either-or thinker. I get easily frustrated and have a hard time living in the present. I don't think it's a coincidence that I have dated five men in recovery who were also working on these issues!

Addicts are also known for "wanting it now," a trait that could be related to their brain chemistry and addictive cravings. This trait can carry over into recovery, causing PIRs to get frustrated and impatient more easily than non-addicts. My friend Paul said he used to get frustrated very easily, especially in the early days of his sobriety. Now, after years of working his recovery program and practicing the "Easy does it" and "One day at a time" philosophies, he said he has more patience and is able to let things roll off him more easily.

If we understand some of the above characteristics, we begin to understand more about why addicts act as they do. After an alcoholic stops drinking or the drug addict stops using, their addictive characteristics don't just magically go away. People in recovery are continually working on themselves—by going to a recovery group, by working the Twelve Steps, by practicing what my friend Josh calls a "recovery mind-set."

The addictive thinking patterns and traits described in this chapter would probably send up red flags for most people in relationships. However, an interesting fact about many PIRs is that, with successful work in their recovery programs, some of their former addictive traits can actually be turned into something positive. For instance, some PIRs who excelled at manipulating now have good careers in sales and marketing; Joe was one of them. My friend Josh worked on his perfectionist tendencies and now has a great job managing a successful not-for-profit in our town. My friend Paul was a big risk-taker, both in his business and in his personal life. In his sobriety, he has established several successful recovery houses in my area. Thanks to the work they did in their respective recovery programs, these PIRs turned dishonesty into honesty, blaming into responsibility, and rationalization into taking charge.

[6]

How
Addictive Traits
Can Affect
a Relationship

MY PIR STEVE and I got to know each other through several organized group activities and events. I had known him for five months when we finally started dating as an official couple (without a lot of other people around), so I thought I was pretty familiar with his habits, likes, and dislikes. On our third date we went to a rather upscale mall that I normally didn't shop at, but I wanted to check out a computer store there. After looking at computers, Steve wanted to explore some other high-end stores. In one store, I stopped him from buying an expensive and unnecessary watch, and in another store, he stopped himself from buying an unneeded and expensive pair of shoes only after he remembered he could get them from a "friend" for less. I didn't want to know about that suspicious-sounding business arrangement, so I didn't ask what he meant. I am a fairly frugal person, and I knew he didn't have a high-paying job, so his impulsive desire to get things he really didn't need made no sense to me. But I was still trying to impress him, so I acted cool and tried not to make a big deal out of it, and we left the mall without any unplanned purchases. That time.

When I became aware of how many of Steve's impulsive desires led to compulsive consumerism, hasty decisions, or reckless actions, I began to wonder if his behavior could be related to his addiction disorder. This was probably my first big "light bulb moment" in our relationship, when I started to understand how deep-rooted many addictive traits can be. Remember, I was coming from a "he's not drinking, so everything must be okay" mind-set, so these insights didn't come easily or naturally.

I now know, however, that some PIRs actually have impulsiveness as a personality trait. Some may quit their jobs with no backup plan, spend money out of control, jump too quickly into relationships, or binge on food or money or clothes—thinking only of their immediate pleasure and not the long-term consequences of their actions. Before many PIRs entered recovery, their poor ability to control their impulses had led them to drink and use. As their addiction disorders worsened, their need for immediate gratification grew. As mentioned in the previous chapter, even in recovery many PIRs like Steve still "want it now"— whatever they define "it" to be. My friend Sandy said that she definitely was guilty of making some impulsive decisions, especially early in her recovery. When I asked her to explain this, she laughed. "It's simple," she said. "I have to do it or have it *now*!" She confessed that she was an impulse buyer who spent excessive amounts of money on things she didn't need. Even now, after many years of sobriety, she knows when she's having an "off" day by her buying patterns. Compulsive spending is a red flag for her that she needs to get things back in balance recovery-wise, or she may risk relapse.

My friend Barb dated Mark. She related experiences with him that mirrored what I experienced with Steve. Barb described how when Mark wanted to buy a pricey item, she'd ask, "Do you *really* need this?" and then they would step away from the store for five minutes to see if he could let go of the attachment to the item. She thought the rush Mark got from his compulsive spending could have been a substitute for the high he got in his using days.

It looks like she was on the right track. Recent studies have found that when shoppers consider making a purchase, a biochemical change takes place in their brains that is similar to the high a user gets from drugs. Their dopamine levels spike at the thought of the immediate reward that shopping brings them. This high will be short-lived, however, which often leads to buyer's remorse when the thrill eventually fades. At any rate, being aware of one's patterns and the reasons why one might buy or act on impulse is good for anyone, particularly PIRs. It's also helpful for those who date PIRs to be aware of these possible tendencies so they can develop strategies for dealing with them, as Barb and Mark did in the example above.

My friend Greg put another spin on this. He came from a very poor and emotionally neglectful family. He had a single mom who had five children to support. He cannot remember playing with or having many toys. After entering recovery and becoming a successful businessman, he impulsively bought cars, Rolex watches, and memberships for spas. He said all that "stuff" made him feel good at first, and then bad afterward. He said he realized he was still trying to fill a deep void that existed since childhood. First he tried to fill it with alcohol and drugs. When he got sober, he tried to fill it with material things. He said that in recovery he realized he had to work on his spiritual and emotional development to help heal the hole inside of him.

Impulsive behavior can factor into a relationship in many ways. As I mentioned in chapter 5, my friend Grace's husband Joe would impulsively decide to make them move between several states in the course of their ten years together. He wouldn't use good judgment; he'd rent office space in the new location before he had any clients, and would keep the office open even after they moved elsewhere. This was a challenge in their relationship until he finally settled down and worked on the underlying reasons for his impulsive behavior.

Steve's impulsive behavior often affected how we made plans for our dates. A couple of times, he and his sober buddies would impulsively and enthusiastically make plans for the weekend. One weekend, it was going to be fishing; another weekend, they were going to golf; yet another time, they had the idea that all of us (PIRs and their dates) could go on a short trip. But most of the time, they wouldn't follow through on their spur-of-the-moment plans. At first this made me nuts because sometimes it involved our plans as well, or we put off doing something together because Steve was supposedly going to be with his friends. I had to learn to let go of expectations and give each new plan several days to see if it went beyond the talking stage or not. Had I known that this behavior wasn't that unusual, especially in early recovery, it wouldn't have thrown me as much.

If you are flexible and you don't mind making last-minute plans or changing to other plans, you might not find this impulsive behavior to be so annoying. Spontaneity works for many people. If you like to plan out your events, however, you might want to talk this through with your PIR and see if you both can come to a workable agreement. It took me a while to get a handle on this with Steve—sometimes we'd "play it by ear," and other times we'd try to plan something. My mantra became: patience and flexibility, patience and flexibility. And, after he realized how his actions could have repercussions in our relationship, Steve tried to be more considerate of me and my feelings.

Learning how to take responsibility as they unlearn old behavior patterns is an important step for PIRs. Many PIRs practice taking responsibility by learning how to properly keep dates and appointments, by learning to manage their money better, and by learning how to successfully communicate the feelings that underlie their impulsivity. These might be totally new skills for some PIRs, so don't expect miracles if you meet him or her when they are fairly new to recovery. It all takes time—and I discovered that my PIR's time clock ran differently from mine.

Time management was a reoccurring issue with Steve, and as a result, he found time commitments challenging. I've since learned that this can also have something to do with a PIR's need for immediate gratification. When PIRs were drinking or using, their perception of time was often limited; they only could measure time as the space between their last drink or hit and the next one. In recovery they are urged to think, "one day (of sobriety) at a time," but most of them have to start with "one moment at a time," and progress upward from there. In the process, they eventually learn to develop patience and not take their sobriety for granted. I read that many old-timers know it's risky to think in terms of years because they can get overconfident and think they've overcome their addiction disorder. This is why even after decades in recovery, an old-timer might declare, "I've been sober 11,315 days" rather than saying, "I've been sober thirty-one years."

But I didn't understand how differently Steve and I perceived time at the beginning of our relationship, so I was apt to get quite annoyed at him when he would arrive late or not be ready when I went to get him. One morning we made breakfast plans, and he was supposed to pick me up. I waited and waited, finally calling him and getting his voicemail. After much worry and another call, I finally reached him—he was working on an extra job in the next county, and had left too early in the morning to call me, he thought. Then he lost track of time and forgot to call later. It was one example of many, and eventually I learned to have a more relaxed time frame if we were just having a casual dinner or doing something fun and flexible. My other strategy was to tell him an earlier pick-up time, or emphasize the importance of his being punctual by asking him to set his phone reminder alarm if we had tickets for an event or something else for which we definitely had to be on time.

Even then, Steve came close to missing important business opportunities because he was so tempted to cancel them at the last minute. It was like something in him couldn't take the pressure of making a commitment to go. He also caused us to be late on several occasions when he went with me to various music jobs. (I'm a professional musician.) And when we finally got to our destination, he was often obstinate, argumentative, and almost childlike in his behavior. I came to learn that I really had to "feel him out" to see if he really wanted to attend these events with me. He would initially say that he wanted to go, but sometimes that turned out not to be the case.

As I mentioned, some PIRs—especially in the first couple of years of sobriety—are so focused on the present day (or moment) that they can't seem to fathom what life will be like next week or next month. When it came to Steve, I learned I couldn't call a week ahead to order tickets to a show or concert because he'd get so anxious and uncertain about the future. He once put me off for several weeks during the run of a show I was in, which I wanted him to come to, so he ended up just not seeing it, period. I had to let that go too.

I had dated another PIR prior to Steve, and even though he'd been eighteen years sober by the time we started dating, he still had a hard time planning anything more than one week in advance. My PIR friend Denise said that her husband, also a PIR, would cancel appointments regularly and totally lose track of time. A couple of times he even took her car without her knowledge, and sometimes he'd be gone for two or three days. She told me that she decided to join Al-Anon after one of those incidents, and said it was so important to be able to talk about this with others who understood what she was going through. Things got worse for her husband, but she learned how to take care of herself despite his unhealthy behavior. Eventually, with the support of Al-Anon and guidance from her Higher Power, she gained enough strength to leave the marriage when she realized he wasn't going to change and that she couldn't continue to live with such uncertainty and disrespect.

I've come to realize that time commitments can be particularly stressful for my PIR friends who have mental illnesses, such as depression or bipolar disorder, in addition to their addiction disorders. Sometimes they just need to cancel plans because they're having a bad day, so I've learned to pencil in our dates and check in with them regularly to see how they're doing. Patience, flexibility, and understanding are good attributes to have with any friends, including PIRs.

In interviewing many PIRs for this book, I found that problems with time generally occurred more often in early recovery. As they progressed in their recovery, these time issues disappeared, or at least became more manageable. My friend Greg said that in his early recovery he actually did the opposite. Instead of being afraid to commit to future plans, he'd overbook himself and fill his calendar. He told me he realizes now that he was still in his "needy" phase, so he tried to do too much in an effort to not disappoint anyone. But he said that trying to be everywhere for everyone left him no time for himself and the hard work of recovery. This reminds us that not all PIRs will have the same issues, and that even if behaviors like impulsivity or time management problems are common, there will be many PIRs who won't bring these traits to the relationship.

Even though I didn't completely understand the connection between PIRs and time issues when I was with Steve, I think I learned a lot by observing what was happening in our relationship. It helped clarify things if I put myself in his mind-set by practicing some of his recovery phrases, such as "One day at a time" and "First things first," which kept me in the present moment. I learned not to obsess so much about the future. I learned to let things go, take a longer view of things, and trust in right outcomes. One time Steve and one of his sobriety buddies were coming to help me fix something at my house, but they were quite late. I was able to let it go and not get upset because I saw the blessings in the situation. Steve had many friends he'd met in the program, and they often traded favors. These friends were very loyal to each other and had each other's backs. I learned that this endearing part of the AA program was actually part of Step Twelve—the service element, where friends of Bill accept and support each other because they share the bond of fellowship. It's another aspect of a recovery program that helps keep PIRs sober. So I look back at that particular morning with a smile on my face, glad that by that point I'd relaxed enough to appreciate that Steve had sober friends who were willing to help him help me. It didn't matter that they were late in doing it.

Many addicts also come into recovery with money issues. As I mentioned earlier, a number of PIRs, like my friend Greg, grew up in struggling families, hearing numerous arguments about money and the lack of money. Others, like Sandy, spent money compulsively, and many fell into debt because of it. In some families, troubles surrounding money involved shame and blame. For example, one PIR's father was a compulsive gambler, and his unenlightened family members told him he'd end up just like his father, which fueled his own gambling addiction. Some PIRs may develop a "deprivation mind-set" and convince themselves they don't deserve to have money. Some may become obsessed with financial security, afraid of being poor like they were as children. Greg told me that he's "horrible" about managing money and if he weren't working his program with commitment, he'd hold on to money out of his deep-rooted fear that he'd squander it. In recovery, he's overcome those fears and has become a successful businessman because he has learned his strengths and weaknesses. He's learned to trust others and ask for help when he needs it by hiring people who have more experience than he does with money.

It's not unusual for PIRs to have debt from their drinking and using days. In recovery programs, they learn to move slowly and cautiously as they begin to take responsibility for paying back what they owe. Some PIRs practice keeping to a budget. Others might start a savings account. In later recovery, they take steps to re-establish their credit, and to manage their money successfully.

I read about one PIR who waited until his fourth year of sobriety to finally begin working on his financial state. He cleaned up his money problems one day at a time, and eventually he found a better job. He read the Third Step every day and learned how to hang in there and work things out, with newfound self-acceptance and belief in his Higher Power.

I also read about a woman in recovery who hadn't yet learned to trust her Higher Power. The more she worried and obsessed about money, the more deceitful she became: lying to a colleague about repaying a small loan, not returning money mistakenly given to her in a bank transaction. She became ashamed and drifted away from her sponsor and the program. After finally hitting an emotional bottom, she remembered a saying she'd heard in recovery: "When all else fails, follow instructions." She asked for help, and she received good advice—and instruction—from some members of Debtors Anonymous. She reworked her Fourth Step inventory and started taking responsibility for her own actions. In the process, she realized that she'd misplaced her faith in her Higher Power (which she thought of as her recovery group). She discovered amazing things could happen when she got out of her own way and stopped trying to control everything.

Before my friend Paul entered recovery, he said he was "crazy with money." He made a lot of it, but he was a big risk-taker, so he said he lost millions of dollars. He also said he was a "big shot in bars," often buying rounds of drinks for everybody. After he stopped drinking, he was broke and broken, and knew he needed to make some changes. He learned how to manage money better, but he still thought being successful meant making back the millions he had lost. At first he struggled to get back to where he had been monetarily, but he eventually discovered that serenity has little to do with finances. Now, years later, he no longer obsesses about money. He is happily married, and he and his wife share an emotionally healthy life that is based on spirituality.

My friend Pam told me that overspending was definitely an issue in the first years of her marriage to Seth. Things became so serious that they separated for a year, and during that time, she created an accounting book so Seth could see for himself how his compulsive spending had contributed to their living beyond their means. She said that the time apart and the simple action of becoming accountable changed their whole financial situation, and put them back on track as a couple.

My PIR, Steve, was very generous with his money, always giving some to guys on the street, always willing to pay for dinner when we went out. The only thing was, he seemed to be broke a lot too. He was behind in child support. He borrowed money from many people, including me, and this was the beginning of the end of our relationship. (More about that in the following chapters.)

Many of the people I interviewed for this book said that money management was an issue that improved as the PIR continued to recover and follow their program. Many of those in long-term recovery, such as Paul, Sandy, Greg, and Seth, have their monetary lives back on track now, and I truly hope that Steve does as well.

I regret that my PIR and I didn't often discuss how we felt about money issues, or even about things in general. His behavior often confused me, and I didn't know how to react, so I'd often choose not to say anything. At other times, I overreacted. Now I know that our inability to express and share feelings is pretty common among PIRs and their significant others.

Almost every PIR with whom I spoke, especially if they were in a relationship, mentioned how working on their communication skills played a huge part in their recovery. One of the characteristics of addictive behavior is the addict's isolation from others. PIRs might enter recovery with out-of-control emotions or be emotionally numb, and many have to learn or relearn how to identify and express their emotions appropriately and effectively. This is especially important in an intimate relationship. In recovery, a PIR works on learning how to trust their partner, as well as how to gain back the mutual trust that might have been lost if their partner was in the relationship with them when they were drinking or using. Step Ten says: ". . . and when we were wrong promptly admitted it." For someone just beginning to date a PIR, it is helpful to know that the PIR is learning how to take responsibility for his or her actions, how to make amends, how to apologize, and how to forgive. Healthy communication is a key to this process, and PIRs are encouraged to get issues out in the open and work them out—which can be challenging for partners who might not have learned healthy communication skills themselves. This is when Al-Anon or Nar-Anon can be helpful. In these meetings, partners learn to hone their own communication skills so they're on the same page as their PIR when it comes to honestly and respectfully talking about feelings and discussing relationship issues.

Early in recovery, there are several sobriety-based symptoms that may interfere with communication. In addition to having difficulty with their emotions, some PIRs have trouble concentrating or remembering things. When I first started dating Steve, he had only been in recovery for one year, and I'm pretty sure that he had stimulus augmentation, which is sensitivity to sight, sound, and touch. At times, he would overreact to music with a certain intense beat to it, becoming increasingly agitated. I quickly learned not to play such music, especially in the car. I have since learned that PIRs with stimulus augmentation may become overwhelmed rather easily. They may retreat, wanting to be by themselves. This could feel strange to someone dating a PIR, as it did with me, but this symptom became less intense for Steve over time.

Due to physical damage from drugs or alcohol, a PIR's

sexual performance may not be "up to par" in the initial stages of recovery, so intimacy may be compromised at first. Most PIRs are aware of this and are advised not to stress about it, as the issue will most likely improve with time. If it becomes an ongoing problem, PIRs may want to ask their physician for advice or treatment. When it comes to physical intimacy, it is especially important to keep the lines of communication open. That way PIRs and their partners can work together to build a relationship based on trust, healing, and mutual support.

In every book I've read and with every couple I've interviewed, the word "honesty" comes up. My friends Seth and Pam said they practice total honesty in their marriage, except when it would hurt the other person. Pam says that her mantra has been "talk, talk, talk." Seth admitted they each have their "buttons" that, when pushed, stir up old feelings from the past about things that happened in their marriage, as well as in their lives before their marriage. When one of these buttons is pushed, they talk it through, reminding each other how certain habits or reactions make them feel. This usually ends up with one of them acknowledging the reactivity and where the feelings came from. They are both very spiritual people and have learned that when one of these "human" moments occurs, they should not take themselves or the situation too seriously.

Pam and Seth are also good at expressing thanks or appreciation for what each does for the other. They remember to compliment each other on something one of them did, or on how one of them looks. They also recognize each other's weaknesses and fears, and are supportive of each other. They both attend a wonderful church that is known for its openness to spiritual growth, and they have a life grounded in spiritual principles. They meditate daily, read spiritual books, and surround themselves with other like-minded people.

Pam and Seth—and so many of the others who have so generously shared their stories and insights in this book—practice the fine art of maintaining good balance and boundaries in their personal lives and in their relationships. This is not an easy task for anyone, especially for PIRs and their partners. But, as you'll see in the next chapter, appropriate balance and boundaries are essential ingredients in a healthy relationship.

[7]

Codependency Is Common, So Healthy Boundaries Are Essential

BACK IN THE LATE 1980S, I was happily involved in my career of music and theater. I was married to a fellow musician I'd met some years before while we were doing community theater. I knew when we were dating that he had some major emotional issues, but I chose to marry him anyway. The following year, we moved to the state in which we still reside, and both of us continued to pursue our careers. In 1989, a colleague of mine suggested I read a very popular book on codependency that had just come out. She even loaned me her copy. I begrudgingly began to read it and found it intriguing, maybe a little too uncomfortably close to home, but not for me. I was happily married! *She* was the neurotic one—she needed it more than I did. I may have had a symptom or two of codependency, but heck, I was too busy tending to my marriage and career to be thinking about them.

Fast-forward a few years, and my marriage had fallen apart. I was smarting from the breakup, emotionally needy, and unfocused. Still, my career was going great, so I concentrated on that. One night I was at a performance when one of my dear older friends, a director with whom I'd done a couple of shows, approached me afterward and expressed her condolences about my divorce. (Word travels quickly in the theater community.) As it turns out, she, too, had recently broken up with her husband. She told me she was attending a group called Codependents Anonymous and asked me to join her at one of the meetings. I hesitated, managing to put her off for a time. But she was persistent and sent me materials that had been helpful to her. I put them aside and never did go with her. After all, codependency was *her* issue, not mine. What was it with all these codependent friends trying to get me to read their books and go to their meetings?

The years flew by, as did many subsequent relationships. Two PIR boyfriends came into and out of my life, prompting me to write this book. My dear friend Seth was one of the first people I talked to about the book. Toward the end of one of our many conversations, he casually suggested, "You may want to include something on codependency." I said I agreed, but thought to myself, "This book is about PIRs, not their partners. *We* didn't cause their addiction disorders. *They're* the ones with dependency problems."

Looking back, I find it interesting that several of my friends saw patterns in me that I never realized were there. It wasn't until recently that I've been able to look objectively at all my previous relationships. I have cried on the shoulders of many friends over the various men who have caused me grief—those guys who lied to me, or who fooled around on me, or who had egos as big as the universe. Then it hit me: these men were all very different, and sometimes they exhibited very different behaviors. But they had one thing in common—*me*—and my behavior. I think I subconsciously chose men I thought I could help. I thought I could "fix" them, all the while ignoring issues of my own that were eerily similar to theirs. This is codependency. Women are known for this, but so are some men. It can affect PIRs as well as non-PIRs. Although it took me a couple of decades to realize it, I am finally starting to get it. "Hi, my name is Karen, and I'm a codependent."

There's a joke in recovery circles about knowing you're codependent if you have a near-death experience and someone else's life flashes before your eyes. Codependency can loosely be described as over-involvement with others. Some critics of the term object to its use because they say it's just another way of blaming those who exhibit admirable qualities such as love and self-sacrifice. After all, aren't we encouraged to be sensitive to another person's feelings and care for them unselfishly? Sure we are, but when these positive behaviors are taken to the extreme, things can get out of balance in a relationship.

Codependents can become so obsessed with another person's feelings and behaviors that they—in an effort to control or "fix" the person—lose sight of what they themselves are feeling or doing. When it comes to addiction-related codependency, a spouse or family member of the addict might get so used to stepping in to help him or her that their identity gets intertwined with the addict's personality and behaviors. While the non-addict isn't dependent on the substance, they seem to be dependent on the addict.

A child of an alcoholic might cover up for Dad if he's too hung over to make it to the family reunion. A child of a drug addict might lie about Mom if she's too stoned to come to a parent-teacher conference. Spouses of addicts may use rationalization and denial to explain away their partner's behavior. My mom told me that my grandma blamed my grandpa's coworkers: "It's those guys from the plant that your dad hangs out with—they're the ones who make him drink." Some family members even blame themselves for causing the addict to drink or use: "If I weren't so critical (or depressed or fat or busy or preoccupied), he or she wouldn't drink or use drugs . . ." Spouses continue to forgive their partners and eventually take over their responsibilities; parents write excuses to the teacher for their addicted child's absences or unruly behavior.

By adopting the same patterns of denial, rationalization, lying, and blame as the addicted family member, the other family members can actually make it easier for the addict to continue to use. In other words, the non-addicts "enable" the addictive behavior to go on without consequence. Enabling can eventually allow the disease of addiction to progress further because it can mask the painful awareness an addict needs in order for them to begin to seek help. If they think their addictive behavior isn't hurting anyone, why should they quit using?

Addiction is called a "family disease" for good reason: it can affect and infect those who come in close contact with it. But, as any Al-Anon or Nar-Anon member can testify, loved ones of addicts are as powerless over addiction as the addict is—no matter how hard they try to control the addict's behavior or the fallout from it. Children and family members may begin to withdraw rather than expose their friends to Mom or Dad and their addictive behaviors. They might stop inviting their friends over for dinner. They often become more secretive. The children may begin to take over for the adults and may develop control issues in adulthood as a result. Family members may even stop communicating with each other, especially about anything related to the problem. I've read that there are two rules in addictive families:

1. Act as if nothing is wrong.
2. Don't you dare tell anyone our secrets.

Codependency is a hard habit to break, and it's quite common for children who grow up in addictive families to exhibit codependent tendencies as adults, which can make it difficult for them to have successful relationships. Many people who are codependent have the following characteristics:

- They change who they are to please others.
- They feel responsible for meeting others' needs at the expense of their own.
- They have low self-esteem, often tied to unresolved shame issues.
- They have compulsive tendencies.

I've read that there's a flip side to codependency, called *counter-dependency,* and PIRs and non-PIRs can be on both sides of the coin. A counter-dependent person can appear to be independent and secure, but will act aloof and indifferent in a relationship—taking, but not giving back. In reality, this person may suffer from low self-esteem, and will often partner with a codependent personality to boost their own ego. This type of partnership can be disastrous, because each person looks to the other to give them what they themselves are lacking. Neither person can meet that hope, of course, and the relationship usually combusts over time.

Codependency and enabling are common character-istics in addictive relationships, and if you are a non-PIR dating a PIR, it's good to be aware of them. You may have come from an addictive family, and may subconsciously seek out a PIR who has had similar family experiences. In my own case, I took my own enabling traits and applied them to both of my PIRs, especially to Steve. I now realize that I sometimes enabled his addictive behavior that was still evident in his recovery, although I had no clue I was enabling. I thought I was just helping.

For example, I loaned Steve money. The first time he asked, I tried to refuse, but he was very convincing. I always had a tight hold on my money, and my rationalization was that this would be a good lesson for me—a chance to prac-tice trust and an opportunity to share my blessings. But I was a mess after I wrote him the check, obsessing about the money until he finally repaid me. The second time he asked, I loaned him money again, and my reasoning this time was that it was an opportunity for me to practice not obsessing so much. Wrong!

I now see that I was enabling Steve—I was making it easier for him to not follow his recovery principles and take responsibility for himself and his actions. I also could have paid more of my share when we went out to dinner. My excuse was that I'd read the popular dating books—I was trying to let Steve take charge and do the "manly" thing. It became clear that he had monetary issues, but I didn't connect the dots between his actions and my own behav-ior until much later. In time I learned that I'm not the only enabler on the relationship block. My friend Barb not only loaned her PIR money several times, she bought him a nice car—and he didn't have a driver's license, which she was well aware of.

I also realize that I became a little codependent when it came to communication challenges with Steve. At times I was too passive, and at other times I was too controlling. Again, it helps to know that I am not the only non-PIR who has done this. My friend Grace described the same passive, yet controlling, characteristics she'd had with her husband Joe. She comes from an addictive family in which no one was very good at communicating their feelings. She attended a codependents' support group, and said that helped her a lot in sorting out her "stuff" from Joe's. My friend Pam had an alcoholic dad who died in a car accident when she was a teenager, and all but one of her immediate family members died as a result of alcoholism, so she is also very aware of her own addictive and codependent traits. She said she learned in counseling how to express her feelings in a constructive way. She also learned better ways to deal with her control and codependency issues, and she said this awareness has made her relationship with Seth much more balanced and healthy.

Now that I have a better understanding of codependency and enabling and see how easy it is for those tendencies to get ignited, I am more confident about maintaining healthy relationships in the future. I hope this knowledge can enrich your own relationship with your PIR. I didn't realize at the time how "letting things slide" could possibly sabotage a PIR's recovery efforts. Not holding them to time commitments, for instance, won't do them any favors if accountability is one of their recovery issues. Overlooking their need to attend meetings or complaining about the time they spend on recovery-related things is another way to undermine their recovery, as is isolating them from their sobriety buddies or sponsor.

My friend Paul told me, "It's so easy to enable if you are in a relationship with someone in recovery. You love them, and you want so much to help them. But you have to know when to say no, when to step out of the equation and let your partner deal with the issue themselves." My friend Greg agreed, and added that he had not been aware of his partner's enabling or codependency behaviors, especially in his earlier days of recovery. Because of his own ego issues, he said he didn't stop to consider how deeply his addictive traits affected her or see how hard she worked to try to keep everything under control and take care of him. Now he said he is able to look past his own issues, and be more considerate of his wife and her needs.

Most PIRs work hard in the first few years of recovery to reclaim parts of themselves that were lost to addiction. They learn more about their true selves and make a commitment to continued growth in recovery. They also learn how to set proper boundaries, so they don't backslide on their recovery path. In a dating relationship, some PIRs are more apt than non-PIRs to become attached too early, so they are cautioned to move slowly. Interestingly, those of us who are attracted to PIRs may also have issues with boundaries. It is important for each partner to allow the other the space and freedom to grow within the relationship.

Setting boundaries is a way to protect ourselves and respect our partner. Simply put, when we set boundaries, we set limits. Appropriate boundaries preserve our individuality and help us keep our self-esteem intact. For a PIR, setting boundaries is crucial to their continued recovery. They must carefully monitor if a new relationship interferes with going to meetings, or setting (and achieving) recovery goals. Some relationships that happen too early in a PIR's recovery can set off a relapse, especially if there's a painful breakup. This is yet another reason why PIRs are cautioned not to start a dating relationship until at least a year into recovery. Setting boundaries is important for you, too, as a non-PIR, so that you can take care of yourself in the relationship.

There are a variety of boundaries that may need to be set before embarking on a healthy relationship. Boundaries can be physical, such as knowing when you or another person is standing too close, talking too loudly, or driving too fast. Boundaries can be emotional, such as knowing when you're too angry, cursing excessively, or being unkind to others. Boundaries can be mental, such as knowing when you're having obsessive-compulsive thoughts, being confusing or spacey, or are unable to have an opinion of your own without someone telling you what to think. There can also be spiritual boundaries, such as knowing when you are being honest, trustworthy, or living life confidently. PIRs might have addiction-related boundaries that help them identify thoughts or behaviors that may lead them to relapse if they cross the boundary and begin using again.

It's essential to pay attention when your emotions and feelings are giving you signals that a boundary is being crossed. It's important for PIRs and non-PIRs alike to recognize if they're being taken advantage of physically, emotionally, or mentally. Certain types of people can set off "boundary alarms." This might be a person who has trouble hearing the word "no," a person who keeps trying to change your mind, or a person who doesn't want to respect a boundary you've set. If you think your boundaries are being compromised (or if you think you might be compromising your partner's boundaries) you may want to ask yourself these questions: Am I able to heed my own "no"? Am I blaming myself or feeling blamed? Am I cutting myself off from friends? Am I being overly critical? Does it seem like I'm always giving in?

If the answers to the above questions set off a warning bell in you, this could be a sign that a boundary is being crossed. I've discovered that my own boundary alarms sound when I'm slipping into codependent behaviors. I'd often ignore a boundary and—because of my low self-esteem or insecurity—continue in relationships long past their overdue date. I envisioned having a certain kind of relationship with each guy I dated, and I fought like hell to make that vision work—even if it turned out to be a fantasy. In addition to ignoring my own boundaries, I'd also compromise my partners' boundaries, eventually losing myself in each relationship in the process.

I can think of two examples of how I ignored boundaries with Steve. After a huge fight, I couldn't let it go when he stopped calling me, so I asked one of our mutual friends to act as an intermediary. I also talked to Steve's sponsor, asking for advice. I finally wrote Steve a big, long, flowery, clingy letter saying how much I missed him. I was trying to hang on for dear life. This eventually brought him back, but not for long. The lack of communication continued, and when I didn't get an answer back for days about a certain event I wanted us to go to, I drove down to his place to ask him in person. This may not seem like a major crime on my part, but I'd gone way past my boundaries and my own sense of self at that point. I couldn't see that this relationship wasn't working. I was clinging to the life raft, refusing to admit defeat, and trying desperately to still be in control.

Control issues are common for PIRs and their partners, especially for those who grew up around the chaos that is addiction. A child in such a household often tries to gain some control in order to make sense of things, and these control tactics often carry over into adult life. Some people in these situations get a false sense of control by drinking or using drugs, eventually becoming addicted to them. The more they struggle for control, the more they drink or use. If the addict is in a romantic relationship, they may assert their control by trying to be the one in charge, the one with the power, because they need their partner to feed their ego and sense of self.

This was the case for Ted. He described himself as a willful, controlling child, and said he carried his manipulating skills into adulthood. He became a salesman out of high school, until his increased drinking resulted in his being fired from one job after another. He said his first three years in recovery were a mess as he tried to tie up the loose ends in his life. Eventually he began to date, but said he found himself needing to control the women he dated. It's no surprise that he said he couldn't deal with strong, independent women. He became stuck in his recovery, having trouble working his Third Step (not a surprise, given that someone who needs to be in control would have trouble turning anything over to anybody!), so he began avoiding his sponsor. He eventually married (ironically, to an independent woman), and finally, in his ninth year of sobriety, he said he "saw the light" after an incident in which he tried to control his wife's shopping habits by trying to throw her shopping bags out the door. Luckily, by that time, Ted said that his wife had become very good at dealing with his controlling ways by gently ignoring him or nicely poking fun at his behavior, making him laugh in spite of himself. She was very strong when necessary, and on the day of the shopping bag incident, she held her ground and did not give in to his manipulations, which allowed him to see the absurdity of his behavior. After this "light bulb" moment, Ted found it helpful to reread *Twelve Steps and Twelve Traditions*. This time he really concentrated on the parts that dealt with the Third Step, which asked him to turn his life and will over to his Higher Power. He attended Step meetings, found a new sponsor, and learned to let someone else do the deciding. He and his wife attended couples counseling, where he learned to let up on his desire to control her, to finally "Let go and let God."

PIRs begin to relinquish control when they work the First Step and admit their powerlessness over addiction. There is a saying that "The surrender stops the battle," and when alcoholics or addicts relinquish control in recovery, they often begin to undo years of manipulative behavior. But surrendering control isn't easy for any of us—and it's especially difficult for addicts. Many PIRs (especially those who struggle with perfectionism) are terrified they'll screw up and make mistakes in recovery if they "let go and let God." In time, and with work, they learn it's okay to be human and make mistakes. I read about a patient in recovery who had requested a pass to leave the hospital to attend a class reunion. The doctor promised him he'd write the pass, and he did, but he wrote the permission on another patient's chart, for which the doctor apologized profusely when he realized his error. The PIR actually had a remarkable improvement after that incident. Before the incident, he'd had enormous fear about being imperfect and making mistakes in recovery, which could disappoint his family once again. When he realized that his doctor, a highly respected physician, could make a mistake and not cause the world to end, he was able to relax and open himself to his recovery journey.

Sheila, a high-powered businesswoman who entered recovery unable to constructively express her feelings, uses the HALT acronym to deal with her control issues. When her perfectionism clicks in and she finds herself falling into old domineering patterns at work, she stops and checks in with herself to see if she is hungry, angry, lonely, or tired (HALT)—the states of mind that, if not addressed, can leave PIRs vulnerable to relapse. One time, even after such a check-in, Sheila said she knew she was close to drinking again. So she got herself to an AA meeting, where she met a woman who had dealt with similar control issues. This woman became her sponsor, and with the sponsor's assistance, Sheila revisited the Twelve Steps, asking help from her Higher Power in again lifting her need and tendency to control.

Learning about control issues, boundaries, and enabling is a lot to digest, but the most important thing to remember is to take care of yourself—mind, body, and spirit—in a holistic, balanced way as you learn about and practice the relationship skills in this book. It is easy when you're dating someone in recovery to have things be all about them.

That's why striking a healthy balance and setting appropriate boundaries in the relationship is so critical, for both individuals and the couple. I encourage you to take time for yourself by exercising, relaxing, or doing something with your own group of friends, or just for yourself. And, if it appeals to you, don't forget to give Al-Anon or Nar-Anon and the Twelve Steps a try. They can help to put the focus back on you, allowing you to be a more supportive partner to your PIR *and* a better friend to yourself.

[8]

Emotional
Sobriety
Is an Ongoing
Process

T HE SETTING WAS LOVELY; the barbecued food was delicious, accompanied by soda and lemonade. It was a joyful celebration, with a deejay spinning lively music. A few couples were dancing, but many people (mostly guys) were standing around the perimeter, looking uncomfortable and acting downright shy and nervous. Even my own date wouldn't dance with me and was acting like a goofball. I was half-expecting a principal to appear and make an announcement that everyone should be nice and dance together.

But this wasn't middle school, or high school. It was a wedding, and the bride and groom were middle-aged PIRs. They'd invited all their PIR friends and their dates, and many of the PIRs were, like my date, fairly new to recovery. I remember looking around at all these PIRs, some of whom were in their forties and fifties, standing around the dance floor, acting like they were still in junior high, ready to jump out of their own skin. And I remember thinking, "What the heck is happening here? Have they reverted back to adolescence?"

"News flash. They didn't revert back," my PIR friend

Mark patiently explained to me a couple of days later when I shared my observations. "They may never have moved forward!" He said a PIR's emotional development often stops at whatever age they are when their addiction takes over. As their disease progresses, a PIR's emotions usually run amok or might become numb from their drinking or drugging. As a result, they often misinterpret their emotions or continue to hide behind their addictive behaviors to cover up what they're feeling—if they're feeling anything at all. When they stop drinking and drugging and enter recovery, they might enjoy *physical sobriety* but discover they are still a ways from experiencing *emotional sobriety.*

In recovery, PIRs who work their programs learn to live life in balance, free of the chaos they experienced when their addiction disorder held them hostage. They practice taking responsibility for their out-of-control addictive behaviors—past and present. When it comes to emotional sobriety, PIRs learn to take responsibility for the out-of-control or distorted emotions (past and present) that may be connected to their addiction disorder. They learn to honor what they're feeling, and practice responding appropriately by acting and reacting in a mature, balanced, and healthy way. They learn to live in the present moment, a day at a time, as emotionally *and* physically sober individuals, no matter what that moment or that day may hold.

Sometimes it takes years for PIRs to realize that their emotional sobriety is not progressing as well as their physical sobriety. This makes sense, because in early recovery they have enough to do just trying to live clean and sober. As a result, a non-PIR could very well be dating a forty-five-year-old PIR whose emotional age is sixteen! This made so much sense to me when Mark explained it. It helped me better understand why my PIR would sometimes act so stubborn, fly off-the-handle, pout like a kid if he didn't get what he wanted *now,* or refuse to dance with me at the wedding by making dumb jokes and acting like a teenager. His use of alcohol and drugs as a teenager had stunted his emotional growth.

Bill Wilson, the cofounder of AA, recognized this same emotional immaturity in himself, years after he got sober. Back in 1958, he wrote a letter that has become a landmark in AA literature. He said that in later recovery those who have the "booze cure" in hand (they've been sober quite a while) come to find that they lack emotional sobriety. He wrote, "Those adolescent urges that so many of us have for top approval, perfect security, and perfect romance— urges quite appropriate to age seventeen—prove to be an impossible way of life when we are at age forty-seven or fifty-seven."[16]

Emotional sobriety means freedom from unhealthy and addictive ways of thinking that trigger distorted emotions. That's not to say that once PIRs are working a recovery program, they will never again act in an emotionally immature way. All of us act like spoiled kids once in a while. As I understand it, the goal of emotional sobriety is to acknowledge your emotions, but process them like any other kind of information your brain gives you. You don't have to react dramatically to your emotions, nor let them rule your life.

Isn't that one of the healthiest things you've ever heard? Shouldn't everyone, PIRs and non-PIRs alike, be practicing emotional sobriety? It is something that I've been working on for years, and I still find it difficult. I can only imagine the challenges PIRs must face when they attempt to deal with skewed emotions related to their addictive behavior, some of which might be surfacing for the first time in years. No wonder many PIRs are challenged when it comes to dating. The first little indication that something may be wrong in a relationship might send them running for cover if they haven't learned to practice emotional sobriety.

In that same letter that has had such a profound effect on so many recovering people, Bill W. also links emotional sobriety with *emotional dependence* and writes about how he looked to others to "supply" him with "prestige, security, and the like."[17] I recently read how some people who have this sort of emotional dependence were often discouraged from freely discovering their own sense of self in childhood. They may have been told that they weren't good enough academically, or that they didn't measure up to one of their siblings. As a result, they didn't grow emotionally, and they carry a lot of shame as adults. It makes sense that many such children then grow up with poor self-esteem, overly concerned with how others view them. They often develop an image of how they think they *should* be and how others should be. They can develop rigid ways of thinking and acting, and also hold others to these standards to keep their shame in check. Like Bill W., they often get so wrapped up in a situation that they overact; they might try to direct or control the outcome, or give in by withdrawing emotionally. Whatever happens becomes "all about them." If things go as they want them to go, they feel satisfied and good about themselves; if things go badly, they feel depressed and bad about themselves.

I have had several students and young friends who, although years younger than me, were light years ahead of me emotionally. I call them my "evolved" students. You can recognize an evolved person when you meet them—they often seem more mature than their years; their energy is peaceful and balanced; and they're easy to talk to and to hang out with. When I've asked them where they acquired this mature sense of self, they usually point to a strong parent or adult influence from their childhood. Of course even these people can have their "moments," as we all can, but it's obvious that they have obtained the tools to quickly put things right when a challenge arises. They take responsibility for their actions and change their behavior when it needs changing. This is something PIRs learn about in recovery. They learn about the importance of monitoring their stress levels, identifying their repressed shame and resentments, handing over their concerns to their Higher Power through prayer and meditation, and making amends as they need to so they can stay on track and not risk relapse.

Emotional sobriety also means you can hold on to your sense of self in a relationship. I heard an analogy on a radio show a few years ago on which healthy relationships were being discussed. The speaker was debunking a sentence in a popular movie of the time, which was "You complete me." He laughed at this and asked, "Then what happens if the relationship falls apart? Are you no longer complete? How much better to think of two healthy relationships as two circles, each separate, which can intersect and come back together at will."

This is ultimately what we all would want for ourselves in a relationship. As discussed in the previous chapter, non-PIRs have to be careful not to enable and also need to be diligent about establishing healthy boundaries. If we're successful, these healthy behaviors can promote our PIR's emotional sobriety. At the same time, our PIRs can mature emotionally by learning how to let go of self-centeredness, practicing humility, and becoming aware when their demands in life are not realistic. They are learning to give the same respect to others that they give to themselves. They are also learning not to take things personally, and to relax their rigid ideals about how someone else's life is supposed to go.

When Bill W. had his insights about emotional sobriety, he dug deep within himself, wondering why the Twelve Steps alone weren't working to relieve his depression. He knew that part of the answer was to take action that took him outside of himself by performing the service work that's part of the Twelfth Step. He experienced emotional sobriety when he stopped relying upon any circumstances, people, or groups outside himself, even including AA, for his own happiness. Freeing himself from outer dependencies allowed him to find the love inside himself, so that he was able to go out and give love and comfort to those who needed it. And even this was done so that he would stay sober, without any expectations for the outcome of his actions.

Many PIRs work on freeing themselves from emotional dependence by making an emotional inventory similar to the moral inventory they did in their Fourth Step. This helps them examine their emotions, dependencies, and unreasonable expectations. Non-PIRs who are in relationships with PIRs can benefit from doing the same. I find myself, as we all do at times, overreacting to outer circumstances and stewing in my feelings for far too long. When this happens, I have some personal sayings and practices that I like to use to correct my course. I am constantly trying to get my ego out of the way, as the ego likes drama and conflict. So if I am feeling irritated by someone or something, I think of the phrase "Don't take it personally," because usually it's just my ego reacting to someone else's ego. I also practice giving a situation "space" by stepping back and trying to be the "observer." Separating my thoughts from the situation often works too. I say to myself, "Here's the situation, and here are my thoughts about the situation." It's always my thoughts that dictate how I feel, not the situation itself, and even if I can't change the situation, I can change those thoughts. And one of my all-time favorite affirmations is "No outer circumstances can affect the quiet peace of my soul." I use that one a lot.

When I catch myself feeling indignant or self-righteous, I remember a funny story about a businessman who always seemed to have mellow employees. If a problem arose and they ran into his office frustrated, he would remind them to follow Rule #9, and they immediately calmed down and soon left happily. When an observer watched in amazement as this very thing happened, he asked what Rule #9 was. The businessman told him, "Rule #9 is 'Don't take yourself so damn seriously.'" The observer then asked about the other rules, to which the businessman replied, "There aren't any other rules." I also use Rule #9 a lot!

I continue to learn about emotional sobriety from my PIR friends. My friend Josh said he often felt like a fifteen-year-old emotionally, and told me how he had to overcome rigid thinking and also fear of rejection in order to become more stable in recovery and attain emotional growth.

He said he was constantly seeking approval from others and avoided confrontation because he wanted so badly to be liked. "My goal was to grow my emotional age so that it eventually matched my chronological age. Only recently have I been able to reconcile the two, with a lot of inner work and a fearless moral inventory," he told me.

My friend Greg said his obstacle to emotional sobriety was his tendency to overreact to situations. He recalled a time when he was at the beach with his family and he became enraged at a man who he thought was taking pictures of the family without Greg's permission. His wife's father tried to calm him down by pointing out that the man was innocently talking on the phone, but Greg's emotions were all over the place. He finally remembered to recite the Serenity Prayer to himself, and jumped in the water to cool off.

My PIR didn't seem to have a lot of anger issues, but many PIRs with whom I've spoken have the same difficulty that Greg had. I've read that the evolutionary "purpose" for the emotion of anger stems from the need to preserve social order. Apparently, over time, human beings developed feelings of anger and outrage in response to injustices such as getting robbed or beaten, or being swindled financially. We consequently developed the capacity to come to the aid of those who suffered these injustices. Managing one's anger is different from stuffing it or repressing it. In many cultures, it is unmanly to cry when one is hurt; therefore, some men may become enraged when someone has hurt them or when they're afraid, rather than crying about it or expressing their fear. Upon entering recovery, PIRs learn that it is okay to feel these things, and many cry for the first time, subsequently releasing a lot of pent-up anger. Learning about the evolution of emotions such as anger helps me to accept them without judging them as good or bad. Then I'm able to dig a little deeper and try to understand why I'm feeling what I'm feeling in a situation, or why someone else might be reacting the way they are. For me, this process is a huge part of emotional growth and maturity.

When my friend Paul was a little boy, his mother told him that his anger would get him in trouble one day. As he grew older and began drinking, he had an especially quick trigger. He did not work on anger in his recovery—he never even established it as a character defect. When he was eight years sober, he had an encounter with an angry woman in a parking lot. His own anger escalated, and he ended up running into her with his car and breaking her ankle. He was sent to jail for one year, and then was under house arrest for two years. It was then that he began working on his emotional sobriety—trying to understand his anger and the frustration in him that led to it. Today, after much work in a Twelve Step program, he has much more patience and does not take things seriously, letting incidents roll off him more easily.

My friend Frank said he has had anger issues since he was a teenager. He described a close-to-perfect childhood, except for the fact that his parents were in denial about his anger problems. He had been a shy little boy, hypersensitive, and easily traumatized, but he escaped those feelings by smoking pot and drinking, which began in the summer of fifth grade. By eighth grade, he was doing this every weekend. He prided himself in his ability to get people to laugh, and used his humor to hide his insecurity. When his first girlfriend "betrayed" him, he said he went over-the-top with anger. He took out his father's loaded gun, drank two gulps of Scotch, and pointed the gun at his girlfriend's head. He then came to his senses, unloaded the gun, and proceeded to smash beer bottles and dig the shards into his hands until the blood ran out. It took him many years, but he finally received the help he needed. In his sobriety (both physical and emotional), Frank said he's finally learned how to be a loving, giving, and kind person. He can express his emotions more easily now, and is a loyal partner to his current girlfriend, Donna. He said he knows that he still has an "intense" personality and that he can be hard to live with. He has moments of great joy, but he also admitted he is not "Mr. Happy." He said he sometimes feels bad that Donna has to deal with him.

In a separate interview, Donna told me that she is naturally a very upbeat, optimistic person, and that she does not let Frank's mood swings throw her off-balance. She has learned to stand her ground and not always give in to him. Sometimes she just allows his "crankiness" to pass, and he eventually comes around and participates in whatever activity they originally had planned. Or, when he says he needs to go into his "man cave," she will go out with her girlfriends and let him be. What keeps them going is that they agree on the important things, they have learned to accept and express their feelings honestly and respectfully, and they have complete trust in each other.

Bill W. found that gaining emotional independence eased the depression he felt when his emotional sobriety slipped and things didn't go his way. When he realized just how much he depended on other people and things to feed his sense of self, he began to practice emotional maturity by living and giving without expectations or the need to control the outcome. Although this worked for Bill and his depression, there are many PIRs who have been diagnosed with brain disorders such as clinical depression, severe anxiety, bipolar disorder, or post-traumatic stress disorder (PTSD) who require ongoing medical attention and treatment. When people have both a mental disorder and an addiction disorder, they are said to have *co-occurring* or *dual disorders*. Some people are born with brain disorders; other mental problems might develop over time or result from some sort of trauma. Often people with mental disorders abuse alcohol and other drugs to "medicate" or numb their mental pain, and this abuse can lead to addictive use. Sometimes alcohol or other drug addiction can even cause a mental disorder.

I read that, in counseling, PIRs are often asked, "Is it a state or is it a trait?" Depression can result from the effects of all the substances the PIR has taken over the years; it can be the result of unrealistic expectations of circumstances (as it apparently was for Bill W.—although there's some evidence that today he may have been diagnosed with clinical depression); or it can be a clinical disorder. Nonclinical depression can also happen as a result of withdrawal. In addition, PIRs in early recovery may present symptoms of depression—such as an inability to concentrate, a low sex drive, or a feeling that life isn't worth living—but these symptoms will tend to decline as the PIR grows stronger in their recovery.

My gentle and kind friend Mark had a lot of anger, especially in his early recovery. He would frequently become enraged at his then-girlfriend Barb, sometimes over something very minor. He was later diagnosed as having bipolar disorder, and he and Barb now think that a lot of this anger surfaced whenever he was in his "manic" mode. Barb says that when he behaved like that, her error was to continue to try to reason with him. Having never been in a confrontational, aggressive relationship, she would defend herself way too much, trying to explain what she meant. She says now she should have just done nothing, walked away, or simply given Mark time and space to calm down.

Fortunately for Mark and other PIRs, co-occurring disorders can be treated effectively at the same time. For some mental health disorders, medications, such as antidepressants, are needed. These aren't addictive chemicals, so professionals, as well as AA and NA, accept that PIRs can take them and still be considered clean and sober. However, as Mark discovered, there is sometimes a dividing line between the old-timers in AA and NA and the younger people where meds are concerned. Believing "a drug is a drug is a drug," many old-timers in recovery resist taking medications, whereas younger PIRs are more open to taking them if they need them. This is why Twelve Step groups like Dual Recovery Anonymous (DRA), Dual Diagnosis Anonymous (DDA), and Double Trouble in Recovery (DTR) are often good options for PIRs with co-occurring disorders.

It is important for non-PIRs who are dating PIRs with co-occurring disorders to understand that just because they treat one problem doesn't mean the other one will somehow just disappear. Stopping drinking or drugging will not cure a PIR's mental disorder any more than treating their mental disorder will cure their addiction disorder. Taking medication and being treated for depression or some other mental disorder doesn't mean they can now drink or take addictive drugs. Mixing most of the medications for mental health disorders with alcohol and other drugs can interfere with the medications' helpful effects and can actually be dangerous. Recovery from an addictive disorder—whether it's co-occurring or not—requires ongoing abstinence.

Mark stopped drinking for several years, but he did nothing else to change his lifestyle. He didn't go to AA or NA, and didn't go to counseling—he just tried to "white knuckle" sobriety. He began working at a very hip restaurant and got caught up in the fast pace of the staff and clientele. Before long, he was drinking again, "like a college student partying for the first time." He and his buddies would party from Friday night until Sunday, and this continued for five years. On nonpartying days, he would drink one quart of ale before dinner. Soon he grew bored with this routine and needed something more, so he turned to drugs as well. Only after he was arrested for soliciting crack cocaine from an undercover agent during a sting did he realize how unmanageable his life had become. He then started attending AA meetings and found a sponsor, but he relapsed after two years. After finally hitting bottom, Mark has now been sober for nine years. He takes nonaddictive medications for his depression and bipolar disorder, and occasionally goes to counseling. He continues to work hard to maintain both physical and emotional sobriety—and it is obvious when you meet him that his hard work is paying off.

When I asked Barb recently about how she dealt with Mark's depression, she said that at first she didn't realize what she was getting herself into. She thought that his depression was just part of his recovery. She began to realize it was something more when, after they'd have one of their frequent fights, he would call and leave not one or two but sometimes up to twenty angry, accusatory messages. At the time, she thought he had anger issues, plus the fallout from early recovery, so she continued to wish for the best.

About a year into the relationship, she found out that he'd relapsed, but she thought that all the anger and lashing out was due to anger at himself for having relapsed. Eventually, she broke up with him. Meanwhile, Mark went back to AA and began working the program again. When it was time to make amends with Barb, they met to talk. She said he looked clearer and more balanced, and when he told her about his bipolar diagnosis, the missing pieces of their relationship puzzle began to fall into place. She continues to be close with Mark and is a main source of support for him.

When I was first dating Steve, I had no clue that many PIRs, especially those in early recovery, have anxiety so severe that they need to be on medication. We had been dating a little over four months when there was an incident in which he became very hyper and agitated. He apologized for it the next week, saying he was trying to go without his anti-anxiety medication. This was the first time he told me about his anxiety, but I wasn't too bothered by the news. I was just glad to know there was a cause (and a remedy) for the situation. Knowing what was going on made it easier for me to support him by encouraging him to check in with his doctor and take his meds if they were necessary.

Mark underscored how anxiety can threaten a PIR's emotional sobriety. He said he still gets anxious, especially when he gets too stressed, and things like moving to a new

residence, monetary upheavals, or feelings of people getting "too much in his business" are red flags that he needs to
work on his emotional sobriety issues (which, he said, can
threaten his general sobriety). Mark reminded me that PIRs
are hypersensitive to change, especially unexpected change.
He said that even the act of attending a different meeting in
a different location can throw him off-balance. New PIRs,
he said, are told that if they start to panic or have an anxiety attack, it is crucial they contact their sponsor or go to a
meeting as soon as possible. The Twelve Step community
can provide a type of comforting "cocoon" that envelopes a
newcomer with unconditional love and support—just the
sort of thing that is needed when a PIR is filled with childlike uncertainty and fear.

If you are dating a PIR who has problems with anxiety
or depression, perhaps you could casually mention that you
are familiar with these issues. Then you might want to gently remind your PIR to self-monitor so he or she can deter-
mine what to do to take tender care of himself or herself.
Barb said that this is what she continues to do with Mark if
she senses his anxiety is on the rise.

As PIRs move from the isolation of addiction to the
richness of living in community, including the service work
they do with other alcoholics and addicts, they move beyond self-absorption to a new awareness and concern for
others. They grow healthy in body, mind, and spirit and in
the process grow up emotionally as well. As Bill W. put it,
they "Twelfth Step" themselves and others into emotional
sobriety.

For those of us who have the privilege to witness this
transformation, "Life will take on new meaning," as Bill W.

said in the Big Book. He wrote, "To watch people recover, to see them help others, to watch loneliness vanish, to see a fellowship grow up about you, to have a host of friends—this is an experience you must not miss."[18]

I could never have predicted how much I would learn and how much I would gain and grow from my relationships with all the PIRs in my life. I once naively thought that recovery issues were *their* problems. Why did *I* need to know about compulsive thinking, dependency, grandiosity, making amends, or emotional sobriety and maturity? Now I realize what a gift these relationships are, and how my own life continues to be enriched because of what I continue to learn about recovery and Twelve Step philosophy. By taking an honest look at my relationships with my PIRs, I have come to understand myself better and I'm more willing and able to take responsibility for my own actions and behavior.

By sharing the joys of recovery and having the opportunity to befriend and support a PIR, I can practice what I've learned and put my own spirituality to work (more about this in the next chapter). It's just like Bill W. wrote—because of my relationships with PIRs and the recovery tools I've gained, "I have been given a quiet place in bright sunshine."[19]

[9]

How
Spirituality
Can Help

ECOMING A "GIRLFRIEND OF BILL" and learning why spirituality is so important to PIRs has helped deepen my own spirituality. In the Big Book, Bill W. tells the story of how he had just about hit bottom, when an old friend and drinking buddy came to visit. This friend seemed lighter and happier than Bill had ever seen him. And, unlike Bill, he was sober. When Bill asked him what was going on, his friend told him, "I've got religion"—which led Bill to conclude that this "alcoholic crackpot" was now "a little cracked about religion."[20] Although he did believe in some sort of a universal spirit, Bill didn't put much stock in organized religion or a God that could allow wars to be fought over religious disputes. But there across the table from him sat his friend, who previously had been as powerless and desperate as Bill still was. When Bill expressed his doubts about this God his friend described, his friend suggested that Bill choose his own concept of God. This was a novel idea for Bill, and it worked. His willingness to believe in a power greater than himself was the first step toward his recovery and the cornerstone of a spiritual program that continues to change millions of lives throughout the world. When he had times of doubt, Bill sat quietly, seeking strength and direction. He came to believe that trusting in a Higher Power, being willing to change the things he could change, being honest with himself and with others, and maintaining a sense of humility were essential to his recovery. This was the beginning of his spiritual awakening.

Spirituality is the essence that connects us to a mysterious presence outside ourselves, which many call God or a Higher Power; the thread that also connects us to others. Sometimes we discover spirituality in a church; sometimes we find it in nature; and sometimes, as with Bill, an old friend knocks on our door and, seeing their obvious joy and serenity, we think, "I want what they have."

I call the summer of 1997 "My summer of spiritual awakening." I was in the midst of my needy, highly codependent, post-divorce phase, but my career was still on track. I had taken a job as stage manager of a summer-long production of *Angels in America,* an intense show that featured many of my crazy actor friends in a very small sixty-three-seat theater. Night after night, the lighting guy, the sound girl, and I squeezed ourselves into a tiny sound booth that we had to access by a shaky ladder. I called about 150 light cues and about 135 sound cues every show. Alex faithfully ran the ancient light board, and Lorna played the sound, using an old reel-to-reel system, cassette tapes, and a primitive mini-CD deck.

We were very close that summer—literally and, soon, figuratively—because there was something that drew us together up in that booth. There may have been an actor portraying an angel onstage every night, but there was a real-life "angel" in our midst in the person of Lorna. She was one of those evolved beings I mentioned in the last chapter.

Not only was she gentle and wise, she was very much into meditation and yoga, and she was studying "New Thought" philosophy—the idea that divinity dwells within each person and that the highest spiritual principle is to love one another unconditionally. Although I was active in a church at the time, I was still searching for answers that traditional religion had not provided. Lorna introduced me to several new books on spirituality that I devoured in my down time, and we had lively and deep conversations up there in that booth and on breaks between shows.

My life gradually changed after that. My church closed due to lack of membership, and I began attending a different type of church that not only answered my long-standing questions, but brought me closer to my personal understanding of a Higher Power. My spiritual path was becoming much clearer. I gradually learned to totally trust in my Higher Power for direction and guidance. As a result, I became a healthier person—emotionally, mentally, and spiritually. Without even realizing it, I was practicing the sort of spirituality that Bill W. happened upon in the 1930s—the same spirituality that my PIR friends who follow the Twelve Steps embrace today.

This spiritual foundation has helped me so much in my relationships with the PIRs I've dated, as well as with my PIR friends. If challenges arise in one of these relationships, I know I have spiritual tools that will help me. And, because I am fortunate enough to have many PIR friends who also rely on these tools and engage in spiritual work, we are able to have deeper and more satisfying relationships. I give my PIR friends so much credit, because many of them had almost no concept of spirituality prior to their sobriety.

Many PIRs with whom I spoke told me how they finally surrendered to their Higher Power. PIRs such as my friend Frank got "sick and tired of being sick and tired." Frank hit bottom in July of 2006. He said he just felt "so beat up." His dad had recently died, and Frank had acted out his grief in addictive ways that brought pain to those who loved him. He realized he wasn't in control of his life, so he reached out for help, and my friend Mark drove him to a meeting. Frank describes the day he took his Third Step as the start of his spiritual awakening. He told his Higher Power, "You give to me what *you* want for me," which was his prayer of surrender and letting go. He describes AA as a spiritual program that can fill a "God-spot," the hole that addiction used to fill.

In the Big Book, Bill W. states that PIRs should not try to convince anyone there is only one way to God. In fact, he and other PIRs were even more open to diverse spiritual paths because they had seen so many examples of how spirituality had positively worked in the recovery of addicts. Today, as in Bill's time, a PIR can call their Higher Power by whatever name they choose. Because of the wide scope of the Twelve Step programs and because of the variety of people around the world who are involved with them, one's own spiritual journey can take many forms. Each journey is ongoing and deeply personal to each PIR. Many PIRs have equated spirituality with religion, as Bill did, but it is not necessary to be of any particular religion to have spirituality. Some PIRs may associate religion with guilt or a judgmental attitude and may not want to become involved with any religious establishment. Others, though, may find comfort in their place of worship. The path is totally up to each PIR. All they need to start on their path is a willingness to accept that there is a *possibility* of a Higher Power. Most PIRs can recall that, prior to sobriety, there seemed to be a power that kept them addicted; so it shouldn't be too big a leap to imagine that an opposite kind of power could come into play in sobriety. As Frank stressed, the presence of this power will begin to replace the void that addiction filled.

The knowledge that a PIR is following a spiritual path may be a scary concept for non-PIRs, especially if they don't consider themselves to be particularly spiritual. If this is your situation, I encourage you to talk with your PIR openly and honestly about it. Ask them about the concept of a Higher Power and how they define their own. Most of the PIRs I know were quite willing, almost excited, to share their spirituality stories. My former boyfriend told me about a "warm, loving light" that surrounded him when he surrendered to his Higher Power. Like him, I believe most PIRs think of their Higher Power as loving, kind, and nurturing—not as scary or intimidating. As I mentioned before, some PIRs view their Higher Power as the positive energy and support they find in their recovery group; others may hold a more traditional idea of a God or spiritual being. It is important for you to remember that this is your PIR's own path. You might be on your own spiritual path and have your own set of beliefs. As with any couple in a relationship, yours and your partner's spiritual paths may not be the same, so it is essential that you communicate in an open and nonjudgmental way with each other. This allows each of you to be free to follow your own path while respecting that of the other.

As millions of PIRs have discovered, maintaining a spiritual program and an ongoing relationship with a Higher

Power helps them stay sober, guides them, gives them strength, and provides new ideas for recovery. Belief in this process takes the focus off the PIR as being the center of the universe, and offers them the assurance and peace of knowing that their Higher Power is not limited by their weaknesses or failures. This knowledge can help them move past their addictive lives and behaviors. Through conscious contact with their Higher Power, PIRs can become hopeful about the future and develop new confidence in their abilities. Learning how to be healthier and more spiritual individuals gives them a head start toward learning how to be more loving, considerate, and compassionate partners.

Step Eleven teaches us the importance of practicing prayer or meditation as a way to quiet and center oneself and stay on a healthy recovery path. Taking some time each day for some quiet contemplation is a way to "take a deep breath" before acting or reacting too quickly or dramatically. This practice can benefit anyone, of course, not just PIRs. And relationships can also benefit if both partners get in the habit of taking time out to occasionally "dwell within" instead of getting stressed or reacting in unhealthy ways that can negatively affect a relationship. My PIR was just beginning to establish a daily practice of meditating, and he loved it.

I can also attest to the power of prayer and meditation. Praying, for me, is a form of talking to my Higher Power, whereas I think of meditating as listening for guidance. I have learned that the act of praying involves much more than simply asking God for a solution to a problem, or asking that we or others might be healed. (Although I do believe that those are good reasons to pray, by the way.) For me, praying is a way of connecting with God. My former minister, Reverend Joan, used to emphatically say, "Get plugged in!" I remember her giving a sermon to demonstrate her point in which she had two bowls of soapy water on a table next to her. She gave her husband Dennis (the co-minister) a manual eggbeater for one bowl, and gave a volunteer from the audience a plugged-in electric hand mixer for the second bowl. Both people then tried to make suds in their bowls. The volunteer's bowl quickly overflowed with suds, whereas poor Reverend Dennis stood there struggling with the eggbeater, soliciting a huge laugh from the audience as he looked sadly at his sudsless bowl. "You can see for yourselves," Reverend Joan said dramatically to underscore her point, "being plugged in gets results!" *Conscious* contact—and, I would add, *continuous* contact—with one's Higher Power works for PIRs and non-PIRs alike. If your colleague at work is getting to you, take a moment to connect with your Higher Power. If someone cuts you off in traffic, turn those "road rage" thoughts over to your Higher Power. Getting (and staying) "plugged in" is hard to do sometimes, but it helps focus your mind on the solution instead of obsessing about the problem.

It is also important for you, as a non-PIR, to stay "plugged in" as you deal with the twists and turns of a relationship with a PIR. Your PIR may occasionally exhibit some of the addictive behaviors discussed in other chapters. It is good to have your own short prayer, affirmation, or saying to get yourself connected to your Higher Power. Even taking a few calming breaths will sometimes redirect your thoughts toward a positive solution. I used to silently say "*Namaste*" to my PIR when he acted out. This word means "I recognize the Divine in you" and was enough to calm me down and help me acknowledge this still-fragile guy and how far he'd already come in his recovery program.

Our minds are almost constantly working—even in our sleep. That's why I find meditation to be such a good tool. It quiets my mind and lets it rest in the same way napping gives my body a rest. Meditating every day for as little as twenty minutes can be very beneficial for stress reduction, mental clarity, and peace of mind. It is especially helpful for new PIRs, as it can aid in clearing out the whirling thoughts and mental cobwebs associated with early recovery. But developing meditation skills takes practice, just like any other skill does.

I start my meditation by playing a CD of some gentle New Age–type music. I sit on my "meditation couch" in my office, with my back and body gently supported. I may read some inspirational material for a few minutes to get me in a more contemplative mood. If I need help that day in solving a particular problem, I will jot the issue down on a pad. I then start to concentrate on my breathing. Sometimes I will do the four/seven/eight type of breathing: I breathe in for four counts, hold my breath for seven counts, then breathe out for eight counts. Other times I just breathe slowly and evenly without counting. Sometimes I'll think of an affirmation or mantra as I breathe. I inhale and think, "I am," and exhale and think, "with God" (which is what I call my Higher Power). Some of my other favorite things to say are:

God is/I am.
The breath/of God.
Thy will/be done.

My goal is to quiet my thoughts. After a few minutes of just focusing on my breathing, I go into a very peaceful zone, where I couldn't have a distracting thought if I tried! I can remain in that space, which is wonderful in itself. Or, if there is a problem I need help with that I wrote on the pad, I do something called the *Japa technique:* you speak the vowel sound that is in the name of whatever you call your Higher Power as you are releasing that issue. For instance, I can gently focus on healing for my cat, and chant out "ahhhhh" (the sound that is in the word "God") and release the issue. This technique is awesome. It's like a deep call to your Higher Power to take the issue from you and solve it—and it works for me. After finishing the Japa technique, I become still again and just breathe. I can almost always feel the presence of my Higher Power during this time. Some people may just meditate on their breath the entire time; others may go into their "God-space" and simply listen. Meditation can take whatever form you want it to take. At the end of my session, I give thanks to my Higher Power and gently open my eyes. Sometimes I'll take a walk or run after this, and wow, do I ever feel connected—to nature, to other people, even to the sky! Meditation can help increase and heighten our awareness and enjoyment of our surroundings, and of life in general.

I think of the type of spirituality and spiritual practice described here as a "spirituality of companionship"— friends accompanying friends, helping, sharing, daring, celebrating, or grieving. It is the kind of humble and pure spirituality Bill W.'s old friend told him about, and the kind my friend Lorna shared with me—the type of compassionate spirituality that invites the deepest forms of human healing. It's not about religion; it's about connection.

My friend Greg explained how important it is for him

to be mindful of that which is outside of himself, and he credits his Twelve Step program for helping with that recognition. He says that the self-centeredness that addicts develop because of their disease is like a weed that takes over their lives, and their job in recovery is to uproot this weed, in the selfless service that is a foundation of the Twelve Step program. "In giving, in being selfless, you can recognize the order, nature, and complexity of relationships," he told me. "In addiction, you have blinders on because of your self-centeredness; the opposite of this is awareness of everything that's around you. Spirituality is recognizing this thing outside of us."

Greg uses meditation as a tool for helping him be aware. He told me a story of the first time that the practice of mindfulness worked for him. He said he was newly sober and was riding too fast on a motorcycle. He was so wrapped up in negativity that he was thinking of crashing the bike and ending it all. Just then, he saw a huge pig standing in the field next to the road, and noticing that animal took the focus off himself just long enough to get him out of the spiral of negative thoughts. He slowed down and eventually pulled up to a fast-food restaurant, where he then became aware of the very nice woman who waited on him. She seemed proud of her work and had a nice smile, Greg said. When he noticed her joy in life, it brought him out of himself. He said he knows in his heart that this awareness is what saved him that day.

Many of the addictive behaviors I have mentioned in previous chapters can be curbed or changed by following a spiritual program. Learning how to stay in the moment, for instance, can help tame the need for instant gratification, the "gotta have it now" syndrome that many new PIRs seem to have. My friends Seth, Mark, Greg, and Sandy all had symptoms of this in their early recovery, and meditating and practicing awareness helped turn these symptoms around. The gung ho, hyperactive behavior that some new PIRs have can also be curbed through the deep breathing and mindfulness of prayer and meditation. Using the popular saying "Easy does it" as a mantra helps too.

The control issues that many PIRs (and non-PIRs) struggle with can be greatly relieved through prayer, meditation, and "letting go and letting God." PIRs are often instructed to do this by putting their problems in a "God-box" if the things they're dealing with are too big for them to handle on their own. For some PIRs, their God-box might be something they imagine. Others might choose to actually write their problems down and physically put the slips of paper in a special box, or burn the slips of paper as a way of symbolically letting go of the problems. Letting go and letting God is good practice for non-PIRs as well. As I mentioned, I use the Japa technique as a way to release my problems to my Higher Power. The point is, once you hand your problems over—once you "let go and let God"—don't try to take the problems back or cling to them! For me, praying for the *right and perfect outcome,* rather than the outcome that I *think* I want—is good for my own control issues. If things are not happening as fast as I want, I affirm "divine order," and allow the steady, unshakeable order of the universe to take the reins.

Sometimes PIRs will recite a prayer at their meetings. The Serenity Prayer (discussed in a previous chapter), for example, is a great tool for releasing control over a situation.

It's worth repeating: *God, grant me the serenity to accept the things I cannot change, courage to change the things I can, and wisdom to know the difference.* This simple prayer has provided great peace of mind for me and many of my PIR friends. I definitely could have used the Serenity Prayer while I was dating my PIR, especially considering what I know now about my enabling tendencies. But at the time, I was flying in the dark—I was clueless as to which behaviors of his (or mine) could be changed, and which could not. Since then, though, I have put the prayer into practice with some of my PIR friends, even as recently as last month. I am learning when to step in and when to back off and let them handle a situation themselves. The wisdom to know the difference is the hardest part!

Also, toward the end of meetings, some Twelve Step groups recite the Lord's Prayer.[21] Several of the Steps are entwined in this prayer. When reciting it, a PIR can acknowledge their Higher Power, ask for forgiveness and the ability to forgive others, and affirm their Higher Power's will for them. However, this prayer, which Jesus introduced as a simple template for how to pray, may be off-putting to many non-Christians, and they may be more comfortable in a group that doesn't recite the Lord's Prayer or in one that uses a substitute prayer. The beauty and freedom of having one's own spiritual path is that PIRs can choose whatever works for them.

Somewhere on my own spiritual path, I came to also think of God as "Great Spirit," the term that Native Americans use. Not to get too deep here, but I believe that this Spirit will give back to me whatever I give to it—prosperity, love, more joy—in even more abundance. But I'm also very careful about putting out negative thoughts to this Spirit, because I think that negativity can grow and come chase me like a boomerang. The value of positive thinking is so important for everyone, PIRs and non-PIRs alike. We all are guilty of negative thoughts, our brains mulling over who might have offended us today, or obsessing about what dumb thing we might have done. (This is different from doing a daily inventory and taking responsibility for our actions and reactions.) If I catch myself obsessing on unpleasant thoughts, which serve me no purpose, I remind myself, "Don't put your attention on what you don't want!" And, of course, the reverse of that is to remember to put my thoughts on what I *do* want.

Recognizing the positive in a situation is something else that takes practice. I have hung out with a variety of people, both PIRs and non-PIRs, who can get very negative in their thinking and conversations. They can be so wrapped up in their immediate responses to a situation that they don't see the big picture. Studying metaphysical practices has helped me. *Meta* means "beyond," so metaphysical means "beyond the physical"—in other words, *spiritual*. Spiritual people know that there is almost always another side to a situation, a deeper meaning than what first appears. In my church we say, "Look beyond appearances." Did you ever find yourself in what you thought was a dire situation, and then it turned out to be the best thing that could have happened to you? You lost your job, but then found an even better one? You broke up with someone, and then found the love of your life? That is what is meant by "beyond appearances." A spiritual person will find "coincidence" after "coincidence." We sometimes call these "God-jobs."

My PIR friends, especially those who have been in recovery for a while, understand this. They have learned to see beyond themselves, and beyond appearances. They, like Greg, learn to trust in their Higher Power to show them the order to things.

My PIR friends and I enjoy saying that we are spiritual beings having a human existence. As PIRs (and their partners) work their spiritual programs, their lives gradually become more manageable. Burdens that they've been carrying for a long time are usually lifted because they've taken responsibility for their actions and made amends. They walk with more confidence, and become stronger and more secure in themselves. They are becoming more aware of the spiritual aspect of their lives. With a lightness of spirit comes the joy of living a sane and sober life. They can laugh at the moments when their "human side" takes over. I recently read a story about how surprised a new PIR was when she found how much laughter goes on in Twelve Step meetings. Laughter and joy are as much a part of a good recovery as the more serious stuff.

My friend Seth is a wonderful example of someone who has grown comfortable in his spirituality. He and his wife Pam try to live their lives as spiritual beings, though they clearly recognize that they have their "human" moments and can laugh at themselves when this happens. Both of them have continued to pursue spiritual growth by reading literature that keeps them grounded in living a life with spiritual principles at its base. They spend time in stillness and meditation almost daily. Seth says that "our lives are less of the outer world and more of the simple life—we have gratitude for the small blessings we see in our lives, a desire to be with others who also are curious about life, and we care about serving others whenever we can in whatever ways are presented to us."

Seth said that service work in the community was a great help in his early recovery. He continues to give back to the recovery community, to his church, and to the community in which he lives. Greg's sponsor told him, "You have a big job, so roll up your sleeves." Greg said that he "uproots the weed of self-centeredness" with selfless service to the community. He says that community service continues to help him be open to and aware of things and people other than himself. Through the company he founded, he has established a recovery program in his town for people in jail. He has gladly sponsored a number of PIRs. Seth is putting Step Twelve into practice by demonstrating that working the first eleven Steps in order can lead to a "spiritual awakening" and that the natural consequence of that is a life of service. He told me, "I may not be the most-liked person, but I am pretty damned loved." He feels he is in the best place now that he can possibly be.

As do I. Addiction is a disease of the spirit as well as a disease of body and mind—a disease that can "trickle down" to those who care for and about an alcoholic or drug addict, wounding their spirits as well. Following my own spiritual path has been the best thing that ever happened to me. I know now that any relationship I enter will suffer if I don't tend to my spirituality with every bit of energy and commitment that PIRs need in tending to their own. I have come a long way from that crazy and life-altering summer of many years ago. To quote the poet Robert Frost: ". . . I took the one [road] less traveled by, / And that has made all the difference."[22] My hope is that all who visit these pages will risk stepping out on their own less-traveled roads to experience the joy of a balanced relationship where *both* partners are healthy in body and mind, and rich in things of the spirit.

[10]

Relapse
Is a
Possibility

WHEN MY FRIEND MARK relapsed and started drinking again about ten years ago, I didn't have a clue he was in trouble. He was working as a waiter at a nice Italian restaurant and doing well—or so I thought. I went to the restaurant with a group of friends for my birthday and Mark waited on us, which was fun. All went pretty well that night, although I remember that Mark seemed tired. What I didn't know was that he was sneaking drinks at the bar between serving customers. Not long after my birthday dinner, he was let go from the restaurant, and Barb (who was his steady girlfriend at the time) told me that he'd relapsed. She was just as clueless as I was. She had simply assumed that he was very stressed from his job. Neither of us was aware at the time that the relapse process begins *before* the PIR actually resumes drinking or using drugs. We didn't know to look for warning signs and didn't know anything about *triggers,* those thoughts and environmental stressors that lead someone back to using. We trusted Mark, and felt betrayed when we realized he had slipped. "Here he goes again," we said, more than a little exasperated. We continued to stand by him, but with less conviction.

This pattern is all too common with PIRs *and* with their partners and friends. However, I've learned that with careful planning and rehearsing—just like when I rehearse for a show—relapses can often be averted. Addiction is a mean disease. It doesn't matter if a PIR has been clean and sober for three months or thirty years; they're always at risk for relapse. When they enter recovery, PIRs are given tools, information, and resources to help them recognize the warning signs of relapse, yet a number of my PIR boyfriends and friends have relapsed anyway.

Circumstances and people change, and recovery strategies have to be adapted from time to time to accommodate those life changes. That's why it's important for PIRs to have a relapse prevention program in place that can be updated when it needs to be. Depending on the situation, partners of PIRs can often help with this—"help" being the operative word. Remember the statement in chapter 7 that said, "Codependents can become so obsessed with another person's feelings and behaviors that they—in an effort to control or 'fix' the person—lose sight of what they themselves are feeling or doing." When it comes to relapse and being in a relationship with a PIR, it is very easy for non-PIRs to lose sight of maintaining healthy boundaries and slip into codependent behavior. We can be kind and caring without attaching ourselves so closely to our PIR's problems that we feel like we are responsible for finding a solution. As you'll see, there are things we can do to help our PIRs avoid relapse and ways to support them if they do relapse, but ultimately, the choices they make are theirs alone. And they alone are responsible for the consequences of those choices.

It is important for both the PIR and his or her partner to

know that relapse does *not* mean failure. Some PIRs might slip up and take a sip or have a toke, even though they've worked hard on their recovery. That one-time slip doesn't have to lead to a full-blown relapse (a return to drinking or using). There's still time for them to step right back into their recovery, and they're not starting from square one when they do. Many PIRs are quick to call themselves losers and give up if they slip, but this does not have to happen. They can stop their addictive behavior by working their program and getting support so they can fix whatever caused the relapse. If your PIR slips, it's important to reassure him or her that their months or years of sobriety are not wasted; their tools are in place, and with all they now know about addiction, they are better able to tighten up their program and make it more relapse-proof.

PIRs can relapse for many reasons. They might reach a "stuck point" in their recovery and find it hard to move forward. Sometimes this involves a past behavior or emotion that they have not really dealt with, such as anger, feelings of inadequacy, or trying to control others. Instead of working on their issues, the PIR may still be in denial about them and avoid dealing with these issues by engaging in other addictive behaviors, such as working too much, overeating or not eating, exercising too much, spending too much, or thrill seeking. These substitute behaviors may bring temporary relief, but they can increase the PIR's stress levels. Eventually their "avoidance system" breaks down, and they may come very close to slipping up. Ideally, they then wake up, realize what happened, and reactivate their recovery.

But if they do not examine and fix what caused them to be stuck, they can repeat the same process over and over again. They will be in "partial recovery"—not drinking or using, but not in a good place either. The Big Book calls this "taking half-measures." "White knuckling it" is another term for exerting sheer willpower to stay abstinent, rather than dealing with the issues that are making a person want to use again. Although these PIRs are outwardly following a recovery program, their lives are gradually spinning out of control. They may also use some over-the-counter substances in their avoidance, including excessive caffeine, nicotine, or sleep aids. Some of these substances may produce anxiety or nervousness, exacerbating the anxiety the PIR already is feeling. The only way PIRs can get themselves out of this rut is to be aware of what is happening and have the courage to dig into the problem and fix it. Looking back, Barb and I now realize that many of Mark's behaviors, such as edginess and insomnia, were warning signs of the potential for relapse. Now I know how important it is to find a quiet time to express concern if a PIR is acting particularly stressed or isolating himself or herself from friends or loved ones. I'm not talking about nagging or confronting; I'm talking about loving, respectful, and honest communication. Since this can be a tricky road to navigate, it is important that partners of PIRs have their own plan of what to do if they think their PIR's recovery is in jeopardy. A good place to gain perspective is in their Al-Anon or Nar-Anon group, where they can share their observations and concerns with others, yet still take care of themselves without trying to control their PIR's behavior or choices.

The road to relapse may start very subtly or even subconsciously, and you and your PIR may not notice anything different at first. The PIR's program may be going so well that they begin to take a little time off from it. They may begin to have some subtle mood changes, not trusting when things are going well, or acting slightly irritable or depressed if things don't go their way. This may cause more unease and some worry, and then denial about the worry. If a partner or family member senses that something is "off" and approaches the PIR, the PIR may get defensive or deny that anything is wrong. Sometimes the PIR may seem more concerned about how others are working their programs than about how they are doing in their own recovery. (I've heard PIRs call this "working the other guy's program.") Or they might get over-involved with other friends' or family members' problems, spreading themselves too thin as a "master counselor" to too many. While compassion and concern are noble virtues, these behaviors can make PIRs vulnerable to relapse if they divert the PIRs from their own path of recovery.

Another early warning sign of relapse that those who date PIRs should be aware of involves resentment—that "number one offender" mentioned in chapter 4; the thing the Big Book says destroys more addicts than anything else. A PIR's unrealistic expectations of themselves and others may lead to a build-up of resentful feelings. The PIR may start talking trash about others; they may say others "owe" them. PIRs may seem self-pitying, excusing their behavior by blaming it on a string of bad luck in their pre-addiction life (not their own poor choices). They might seem negative and pessimistic. These addictive thought patterns that are common in recovery were called "stinkin' thinkin'" by the old-time AA members. They also coined the term "dry drunk" to describe an alcoholic who doesn't drink, but retains the behaviors and thought patterns of an active drinker.

My friend Josh calls this type of behavior "false recovery." Josh went to rehab for drugs in his early thirties. He told me he'd gotten into some legal trouble and made a plea with God to help him stop using and drinking. He sobered up, but did not fully embrace the ideas of Twelve Step recovery programs. He said he wasn't using drugs, yet he still had addictive behavior. He said he did not totally buy into the idea of a "recovery mind-set" until he turned forty, and he is now totally committed to his Twelve Step program.

A sure warning sign for a potential relapse is when a PIR starts seeking out old friendships from his or her drinking or using days. They might decide enough time has passed that they can comfortably see an old drinking buddy, or an old friend with whom they used to shoot up. PIRs may have feelings of invulnerability, thinking they can once again attend parties where there are substances being used, or go to some of their old haunts, without negative consequences. Even with an AA or NA buddy along, even with a "script" to stick to in case the PIR is offered a drink or a substance— this is still risky behavior.

PIRs on the road to relapse may conveniently forget how sick the booze and the drugs used to make them, and what fools they made of themselves when they used. If your PIR starts talking fondly of the "good old days" (sometimes called "romancing" the drink or drug or living in a "pink cloud"), you might want to gently explore if they're feeling like they want to drink or use again—then talk about what measures they think they can take to prevent a relapse and how you can support them.

My friend Frank compares recovery and being vulnerable to relapse to having a broken leg that never heals until it's set properly. As mentioned previously, Frank had anger issues as a teenager, along with his addiction to alcohol and drugs. At age twenty-six, he entered an outpatient rehab program and was sober for over eleven years, although he told me he didn't fully believe in the recovery program he was supposedly working. He was also in therapy but didn't commit to it. Although he wasn't having the severe anger episodes, he said he was still "living dangerously" by putting himself in precarious situations that threatened his sobriety. He somehow managed to stay sober even though he worked in a bar.

What undermined his sobriety even more was a relationship with a fellow alcoholic who was hiding bottles and in denial about her own addiction. The anger that he'd never worked on resurfaced in that relationship. He said he felt like he became "addicted to her," by getting over-involved in her problems and trying to "save" her, but he was not "walking the talk." Craving her attention, he described how he used intimidation as a power play to get an emotional reaction from her. He told her "I can f--king do this too" and tried to show her he could drink a beer, then go to a meeting. But, of course, it didn't work out that way—he ended up buying one, then two six-packs and getting as wasted as she was. He finally realized what he was doing, got out of the relationship, and re-entered the program, this time taking recovery seriously and working diligently on his anger *and* on his codependency issues.

Often, by the time PIRs get to the point of relapse, their heads are so full of a jumble of addictive thoughts that they don't even realize the trouble they're in. If your PIR has been following their program faithfully, they should have a contingency plan that they set up in early recovery to ensure that they won't get to that point that Frank and other PIRs I know did. A good relapse prevention plan should include a list of reminders about situations that triggered episodes in the past, such as breaking up with one's boyfriend or girlfriend. It should list early warning signs the PIR experienced in the past, and triggers that may come up again.

Certain triggers that involve the senses may come up in the everyday life of the PIR, which could lead to relapse. An example of this might be something the PIR sees, such as a television ad for beer, or a line of powdered sugar someone spilled on the kitchen counter. An auditory trigger might be a song the PIR listened to back in their using days. Smells can also bring back all sorts of memories. For instance, whenever I smell stale air-conditioning and a particular kind of industrial cleaner used in restaurants, I'm immediately taken back to the days when I did non-union dinner theater in musty old supper clubs—some of my best (and worst) memories! For PIRs, certain smells may bring back memories of the days they spent drinking at the bar. Even something the PIR touches—such as leather, which could remind them of a jacket they used to wear in their partying days, or the smooth top of a coffee table, which could bring back memories of their cocaine days—could be enough of a trigger to set off a relapse. As part of their relapse-prevention plan, the PIR can work to predict and prevent these ahead of time. It can be very helpful to your PIR if you are also aware of his or her triggers, so communicating openly and honestly with your PIR about them is important and can help prevent a sobriety-threatening situation.

Good times may also trigger a relapse. PIRs learn to be very cautious during holidays, birthdays, and anniversaries, as old memories may be stirred up that may put them at risk for a relapse. Certain celebratory milestones in the PIR's recovery are reason for joy, but also for caution, as the PIR may let down their guard after passing a notable anniversary, triggering the road to relapse. My PIR friends tell me that the riskiest anniversaries seem to be the three-month, six-month, and one-year levels, but PIRs know that any anniversary is to be both celebrated and heeded. Those people who are dating PIRs may want to take note of these special dates so they can talk about their significance with their PIR and get a sense of how he or she is handling them.

The PIR may not be aware of the early warning signs, but, as time goes on, these signs can lead to serious and more obvious signals that are red flags for potential relapse. Red-flag behaviors are treated like an SOS—they are signs that sobriety is already seriously compromised. Some of these include:

- Lying. The PIR may concoct stories about why they missed a meeting or a doctor's appointment. They may be dishonest with themselves and those around them, forgetting that honesty is the primary factor in preventing relapse.
- Blaming others for their own problems, not taking responsibility for their own actions and behavior
- Experiencing anxiety and panic attacks that have previously been under control
- Acting out compulsive behaviors (eating disorders, promiscuous sex, gambling)
- Avoiding commitments

- Not following the program—not making amends when they're called for; not doing the personal daily inventory called for in Step Ten
- Wondering if it really was the drinking or using that was the problem; entertaining thoughts of drinking or using socially once again
- Isolating oneself; not checking in regularly with one's sponsor
- Not taking care of personal hygiene
- Considering switching to a different substance—for instance, if the PIR's drug of choice was pot, they are now thinking of having a drink
- Exhibiting denial about any of the above, or denial about other problems in the PIR's life such as money, relationships, or work problems

My friend Greg's road to relapse started with his continued thinking about the girlfriend with whom he'd done drugs. This addictive thinking was a red flag for him. Another red flag was that he started to go back to their old hangouts, even though she wasn't there. He ended up escaping to South Florida, and staying on a wealthy family member's sailboat. In six months' time he attended only two meetings—his excuse was that he didn't feel the connection with the members. Around this time he was also feeling ill, and took some of his money out of savings, giving three $100 bills to the first person he saw who could get him drugs. He eventually realized the error of his ways, moved back home, and got himself back in the program.

The old saying "an ounce of prevention is worth a pound of cure" makes sense when it comes to relapse prevention.

In addition to listing the emotions, behaviors, and high-risk situations that can lead to relapse, a PIR's emergency relapse plan should include:

- the people or places they can call for help (sponsor, supportive family member or friend, treatment center)
- the places they can go to for help (meetings, sponsor's house, treatment center, therapist)
- a list of consequences of drinking and using that will motivate them to prevent relapse (loss of family, friends, career, health)
- a "last resort" contract; for example, "If I am unwilling to follow this plan, I agree to check into a treatment center, move out of the house, go to detox, etc."

PIRs should give a copy of this plan to their sponsor and family members or friends who support their recovery so the supporters will know what to do to help them. I think it's a good idea for a PIR's significant other to have a copy of the plan, because he or she is often the first one to notice behavioral changes. Of course this isn't something you de- mand in your days of early dating. (It isn't something you'd *demand* at all.) But if dating turns into a more serious re- lationship, you might want to find a good time to ask your PIR if they have a relapse prevention plan. Ask them also if they have a volunteer to support them in putting the plan into practice (to the extent they're willing to share their plan with you). Be very clear with your PIR what your role is and what it isn't. You are *not* the PIR's counselor or sponsor—it is the PIR's responsibility to develop and follow their plan and to reach out to their sponsor, counselor, or group for help if the need arises. Your role is to offer support and honesty in communicating to your PIR how their behavior may be impacting you. Now is the time to establish what your own boundaries will be, in case you see warning signs of relapse. It can be easy to get too involved with monitoring warning signs and red flags, especially for those of us who struggle with codependency. If you see an issue arising, you could gently mention it and then back off, letting your PIR take it from there.

If your PIR has shared with you the triggers, risky situations, emotions, and behaviors that can make him or her vulnerable to relapse, you can support your PIR by asking if it would help to brainstorm some strategies to counteract those risks if and when they arise. Monitoring stress, for example, is very important in recovery, as high stress levels can lead to relapse. Addictive behavioral tendencies that can exacerbate stress include perfectionism, impatience, obsessive worry, and mistrust. The presence of any of these behaviors should send up red flags.

My friend Josh said he had to be very mindful of stress for the first three years; he gradually learned how to handle stress through meditation, prayer, and practicing awareness. Being aware of stress is very important for someone dating a PIR. Noting when a situation may be stressful for your PIR, and taking action to alleviate it, will be better for both of you. My friend Beth says that she and her PIR learned to step away from a stressful situation and give it some distance. When they returned to it, she said the situation never seemed as dire. Reciting the Serenity Prayer can help relieve stress for PIRs and non-PIRs alike, as can the HALT acronym (do not allow yourself to get too *hungry, angry, lonely,* or *tired*).

My PIR sometimes became easily overwhelmed by the simplest thing, such as running errands or making decisions. He would also get tired quickly, sometimes going from periods of great frenetic activity to extreme tiredness all in less than an hour. When this occurred, his concentration level was usually shot as well, and it was time to call it a day. I wish I'd known at that time about the HALT rule and how careful PIRs need to be about not overdoing. I could have let my PIR know more directly how those behaviors affected me and offered some suggestions, such as practicing his meditation and relaxation techniques or continuing to pray and read spiritual, uplifting literature.

Sometimes outside circumstances can weaken a PIR's defenses. Situations such as a job loss, a divorce, or an illness can cause a relapse. When PIRs become sick, they need to be especially vigilant with their doctors. They are advised to emphasize to their health-care professionals that they are addicts and they have to be very careful about taking addictive drugs for an illness. If the drugs are absolutely necessary, such as prescription painkillers for surgery or an injury, it's suggested that the PIR ask if there are any alternatives that would be just as effective. If there aren't, then he or she can ask for the minimum dose, and the shortest possible time frame for administering medication, with vigilant monitoring by their health-care team. My friend Mark recently came through a serious illness for which narcotic painkillers were prescribed. He notified the hospital doctors of his addiction history, and they tried to give him the smallest dose that would work. His whole "team" (his doctors, nurses, friends, and family) continued to watch him closely for signs that he could be hooked, and we all breathed a sigh of relief when he took the last of his prescription.

As noted in chapter 8, change can be very stressful to a PIR, and they are cautioned not to make any unnecessary changes in the first two years of recovery. If a change is necessary, PIRs are cautioned to carefully plan and monitor their actions and reactions regarding it—something their significant other might be able to help them with. I think it's important for PIRs at any stage of recovery to be ultra-cautious about change and the stress that can result from it. My friend Mark now knows that his relapse was triggered by too much change, too quickly. He'd been in the program for three years and he was feeling overwhelmed. His dad had a heart attack; he had issues with his brothers and step-brothers; he was trying to go back to school and was also looking for a job. His life and his thoughts were getting out of control. His stress levels were very high.

Even with an emergency relapse recovery plan in place, PIRs can slip up, but the sooner they realize that one drink or hit does not automatically deserve another, the better off they will be. PIRs who survive relapse learn that it's important for them not to say "I slipped, so what's the point? I've blown it, so I may just as well keep on drinking and using." The point, as mentioned earlier, is that they can get back on track, call their sponsor, go to a meeting (every night if they need to), and revisit the Steps. With full-blown relapse, it can take much less time to hit bottom than it did the first time they sobered up and entered recovery. And they may fall even harder than they did that first time.

But relapses happen—sometimes even more than once. If a PIR does indeed relapse, it is still crucial that they know it is not the end of the world. It took some of my PIR friends a few times before recovery really took hold. But recovery did finally set in, and they continue to stay clean and sober, one day at a time. Depending on how long and how severe a relapse is, a PIR may need to detoxify in a hospital, even if they didn't need to the first time, as many withdrawal symptoms can be worse the second time around. After detoxification, they may need professional help, even if they didn't get this before. I have heard from several PIRs who relapsed that this was a big wake-up call for them. As one of them told me, "This time I took it seriously. I listened to my counselor and was more open to what she told me."

My PIR friends who have relapsed told me that it's very humbling to admit to themselves and others that they did not know all there was to know about staying sober. In order for them to stop the recovery/relapse cycle, they said it was essential to "restart" their program, looking carefully for the gaps in their previous plan and plugging those gaps with a plan for putting recovery principles into practice each day. They said that, although it took less time to complete their Steps after relapse because they knew what was expected of them, it was still essential to take things seriously and diligently rework every Step.

After relapse, a PIR's loved ones who were initially encouraged by the PIR's progress the first time around may show their hurt and disappointment by being angry with the PIR, like Barb and I were with Mark. This is a perfectly understandable and normal response. Relapses can be devastating for everyone concerned. If your PIR relapses, it is important for you, too, to know it's not the end of the world for either of you (although if the PIR doesn't take corrective measures, it could mean the end of the relationship). PIRs don't "flunk" recovery when they relapse. They made a mistake and took a wrong turn, but that doesn't mean they can't get back on the road to recovery. That said, it is very hard to watch someone you love relapse. If your PIR has relapsed, you may be angry and feel betrayed. You can honestly tell them how you feel and the effect their actions have had on you. You can also set limits and let them know what these boundaries are, remembering that you also can't control how—or even whether—they hear you. If they're still in a "relapse state of mind," they might try to use your anger or reactions as an excuse to continue drinking or using, but that's not your problem. Or responsibility. Or fault. If this happens, it's a good time to reread Step One, reminding yourself that you are also powerless over alcohol and drugs and how unmanageable your life can get when someone you love is in the throes of addiction.

Remember: you can't save your PIR and you can't make them get help. It is up to *them* to change their behavior. But you can help yourself. In Al-Anon there is a saying: "You didn't cause it, you can't control it, and you can't cure it." As mentioned earlier in this chapter, it is essential that you, too, have a contingency plan in place in case your PIR relapses. It is a good idea to have a list of people you can call for support—trusted friends, a spiritual advisor, your Al-Anon or Nar-Anon sponsor. Even if your PIR hasn't yet rebounded, go ahead and do the Steps for yourself. Go to your Al-Anon or Nar-Anon meetings—double up on them if you can. Going to the meetings will help you practice healthy detachment. Go back through your own personal inventory and make sure you are monitoring it. Take good care of yourself—exercise regularly, eat healthy foods, meditate daily, and stay connected to your spiritual life. Trust that, one way or another, this too shall pass. And if it doesn't pass and your PIR does not rebound, a solid, healthy plan for yourself will benefit you even more, especially since such a plan can provide you with distance and perspective on the situation. You may need to make some difficult decisions about whether or not you intend to stay in a relationship with an addict who is back to drinking or using and won't get help.

If a PIR relapses, those who are close to him or her fervently hope that their PIR can renew their program with honesty and a positive attitude—that the knowledge they had in recovery prior to their relapse is not wasted and can be put to use once again. Research shows that those who view relapse as a serious but alterable mistake restart their sobriety and achieve abstinence sooner.

Mark went on to have a successful recovery after his relapse. He redid his Steps, he renewed and repaired his relationships, and he continues to watch his stress levels. He is careful not to isolate himself and takes care of himself emotionally, physically, and spiritually. He did not flunk sobriety. He learned from his relapse, and continues to successfully follow his recovery program. Mark discovered what Ernest Hemingway meant when he wrote, "The world breaks everyone and afterwards many are strong at the broken places."[23]

From what I've observed and learned from my PIR friends, whose wisdom I cherish and whose courage I so admire, PIRs can grow not just strong, but *stronger* when relapse threatens to break them and they survive and even thrive in its wake. And I've also learned that those relationships that survive relapse can also grow stronger if *both* partners do the following:

- work their individual spiritual programs
- practice good self-care by setting and honoring boundaries
- treat each other with respect
- communicate openly and honestly
- take responsibility for their own actions and reactions

[11]

You Can Still Have Fun on Dates

I HAVE TO ADMIT that when I met Ron, my first PIR, I had no idea how to act with him on a date. I knew he'd been a drug addict and an alcoholic, and that he'd been sober for eighteen years. I didn't know if I could drink in front of him when we were having dinner. I didn't know what I could, and couldn't, cook for him. I wasn't sure what types of restaurants we could go to.

Thankfully, he was very good about guiding me through this. Our first date was at a lovely indoor-outdoor restaurant right on the beach. He drank iced tea, and I had a ginger ale, but he said it was fine if I wanted to have a glass of wine. As we ate, he gave me a little background about his addiction history, and because he'd been sober for quite a while, I tended to think of his addiction as a nonissue. Our relationship lasted a couple of months, fueled initially by our similar views on spirituality. We attended each other's churches and shared some books on spiritual matters. He came with me to a couple of my shows, and enjoyed them.

We gradually realized, however, that we were not right for each other in other ways, and we ended the relationship on a friendly note. By then I had seen a hint of past addictive behaviors in some of the things he was doing, but our relationship just didn't last long enough for me to question them. I felt, though, that I had a good "tryout" with him and learned some pointers about what to do and how to act around a PIR. I still didn't know too much about addiction or recovery, though, so I couldn't fully appreciate all that PIRs go through to reach the point where they feel good enough about themselves that they can relax and have fun on dates.

Knowing what I know now about the process of recovery would have been really helpful when I began to date Steve. Steve and I began our relationship saga surrounded by other people in the singles group my girlfriend and I started in our AA-friendly church. We planned several fun group outings, including a guided turtle watch on the beach and going to the weekly outdoor concert series in town. I got to know Steve better because we both kept attending those singles events. Pretty soon I asked him to one of my shows and also to a weekly gig I was doing at the time. We were still just friends at that point, until maybe a month later when we both realized we really liked each other.

It was easier to get to know Steve because we started out as just friends, doing group activities. If you want to get to know your PIR gradually like I did, try starting out slowly, having your first date or two be at a coffee shop or casual diner. Recovery group members will often go out for coffee after meetings, so such places would probably be familiar to them and more in their comfort zone. As with any new date, you want to be in an environment that is conducive to conversation so you can get to know each other better. I advise keeping the conversation light and easy when you first begin dating. Save the deep, intimate conversations for later. Most PIRs I know say they didn't mind telling their dates some general information about their recovery history, such as how many years of sobriety they have and if they are active in a Twelve Step program. But try not to interrogate them about their using days or their recovery. They can share more when they're more comfortable with you and, if they haven't been sober long, more solid in their recovery.

Steve's and my first official date was to a local diner he liked. I asked some of my other PIR friends, as well as their non-PIR partners, where they went for their first dates and found out that Joan and Jack went to a museum; Frank and Donna's first "official" date was to a sushi restaurant (although Donna had hung out with him and his band mates at several gigs prior to that); and Seth and Pam went to an AA meeting! (Nothing like introducing your girlfriend to your program right off the bat!)

If you and your PIR continue to date, you can branch out to other places and restaurants. I've learned through mistakes to now be very straightforward with PIRs instead of guessing if they are comfortable with a certain setting. Everyone in recovery is different, so their comfort levels, of course, will vary. Factors include how long they have been in recovery, what their triggers are—what sights, sounds, and smells would remind them of old haunts and behaviors— and, of course, if they like the type of food served at the restaurant! Personally, I would not have chosen several of the restaurants that Steve and I went to had I known what I know now. I suggested places like sports bars, and I now think that Steve was not cool with this, but he didn't want to tell me. The Big Book states, "So our rule is not to avoid a place where there is drinking, *if we have a legitimate reason for being there.*"[24] But Steve was just one year and five months into recovery when we started dating, and I think we could have gone to places where alcohol wasn't a prominent feature.

I've learned that the main thing is to be honest and open with your date, and urge them to be honest with you if a certain type of restaurant or venue may bother them. My friend Sandy says she tells people in recovery to "check your motives." "If you're sitting at a bar because you have some friends that drink and you want to be social with them, that's one thing. If you sidle up to the bar and have, say, a glass of ginger ale with ice in a rocks glass, by yourself, that is something totally different," she said. She is implying that the latter is part of the PIR's addictive behavior, whether or not the PIR is drinking alcohol.

Among other things, recovery is about replacing old, negative, stressful habits with positive, happy, healthy ones. PIRs have to learn (or relearn) what it means to have a healthy lifestyle. As emphasized throughout this book, recovery is about healing minds, spirits, *and* bodies. Some PIRs neglected and even abused their bodies when they were drinking or drugging. Many of them have no clue how to eat properly, and others have to re-educate themselves about good nutrition. They are encouraged to plan their meals so they don't get too hungry, as hunger can bring on stress, and too much stress can make them vulnerable to relapse. (Remember the "HALT" acronym.) Snacks throughout the day are good for stabilizing blood sugar. Monitoring caffeine intake is also important because too much caffeine can make anyone nervous and anxious. Making time to eat slowly, staying in the moment and enjoying food, is also important. For a PIR new to recovery, it can take a while to get used to that practice, so it helps to eat in an environment that is fairly quiet and not overstimulating.

These practical ideas are good to remember when you are planning dates with your PIR, and they are things that can benefit both of you—or anyone who wants to adopt a healthier lifestyle. My PIR friend Frank has taken good nutrition one step further by becoming quite the gourmet chef. He learned in recovery how important good nutrition is for PIRs, and he has been fixing healthy meals for himself and Donna for quite some time. Recently he took yet another step and became vegan, saying that he has more energy and enthusiasm now than ever before. When our friend Mark went through his health challenge recently, Frank and I cooked some healthy vegan meals for him using legumes, vegetables, and greens. Mark wasn't sure about all this "new" food at first, but later he came to like it so much that he joked, "I should get sick more often!"

As Steve and I continued dating, I occasionally would make dinner for us at home—a good way to eat healthy in a quiet and comfortable environment. Luckily, my PIR friends counseled me on what to make. There are some ingredients that many of us would not give a second thought, but we need to rethink some of these ingredients if we are cooking for someone in recovery. Here is a list of the obvious ones:

- Anything cooked with wine, beer, or spirits, especially if the alcohol has not cooked off and you can still taste it.

- Tiramisu or similar desserts with alcohol in them. Also certain prepackaged holiday items like fruitcake or Zabaglione.
- Anything flavored with a definitive liquor taste, such as Kahlua-flavored coffee creamer, or rum raisin ice cream, as these can trigger a craving.
- Vanilla extract and other flavorings for cooking. Try to find flavorings without alcohol.

I initially had some other condiments on this list like red wine vinegar and Dijon mustard, but my friends Paul and Sandy said those were no big deal—they laughed when I said I was checking labels. They were the ones who mentioned tiramisu, and they also mentioned mouthwash and Nyquil as things to avoid. (Not that I would cook with these!) As mentioned throughout this book, each PIR is different, so check with your partner for what their triggers may be.

You might wonder if *you* can drink while your PIR can't, or if drinking in front of him or her might trigger a desire to use on their part. I sigh as I write this, because, looking back, I think I screwed up in this regard. Steve was very early in his recovery—I could have gone without a glass of wine at dinner, especially early in the relationship. Yes, he said he was fine with my having a glass of wine, but even so, I didn't really think about *his* feelings that much. It wasn't really a necessity for me to have wine to enjoy my meal and the evening. I didn't realize how vulnerable he still was. If your PIR is in long-term, stable recovery like my PIR Ron was, it should be okay to have an alcoholic beverage at dinner, but I would be hesitant, knowing what I now know, to drink in front of someone relatively new to recovery (under two years, according to Paul and Sandy). The important thing is to be open and honest with your PIR—and for them to be open and honest with you.

One of my non-PIR friends, Joan, recently realized how important it was to have this discussion with Jack, her PIR. At the beginning of their relationship she was ultra-cautious about drinking in front of him, even though he was sober fifteen years by the time they'd met. She promised him she'd never have liquor in her house when he was there. After several years of dating and seeing how stable he seemed in his sobriety, she relented on this promise and now has wine and beer in the house. (They have separate residences.) She was recently surprised when he became angry about this. I suggested that it probably wasn't the fact that the booze was in the house, but that she'd gone back on her promise. I told her, "Keeping one's word is a badge of honor with those in recovery; we who are not in recovery are told to hold PIRs to their word, so why would the opposite not be true as well?" I hoped I was not presumptuous in mentioning this, but it seemed to make sense to Joan, who had a little "aha" moment at that point, and has since discussed the situation honestly and lovingly with Jack.

You might also wonder if you can take your PIR to a holiday, office, or birthday party, or to a wedding where alcohol will most likely be served. I think that, depending on how long they've been in recovery and their comfort levels, most PIRs will probably be okay with going to parties and other events where people are drinking. However, it's best to confirm with the host or hostess ahead of time that there will be nonalcoholic beverages available such as soda and juice. If punch is served, you'll want to be sure to check if it has alcohol in it and give your PIR a heads-up if it does. You can also discreetly inquire if any of the foods contain alcohol so your PIR can avoid those. Many PIRs I know ask for soda or juice right away and keep their glass with them at all times to reduce the temptation of someone offering them a drink. I think it's also a good idea to arrive on time, and not to plan on staying too late when partygoers might get rowdy if the liquor flows more freely.

Speaking of late-night dates—PIRs who are new to recovery may find that their sleep systems may be out of whack for a while, so it's good to be sensitive to this fact if their energy level doesn't match yours. A regular exercise program can help with this—and is another thing that can also benefit partners of PIRs. Exercise is important for rebalancing brain chemistry. Remember from chapter 2 that the addict's brain stops producing "feel good" chemicals like dopamine because addicts have been substituting alcohol or drugs instead. Once the PIR is sober, his or her brain will take some time to begin producing dopamine and other mood-related brain chemicals on its own. Exercise can help stimulate production of dopamine, which can help reduce depression and anxiety levels. Staying active is also excellent for reducing stress and strengthening the body, and there are so many different and fun ways to exercise. This may be a difficult transition for many alcoholics and addicts, however, since exercise and other healthy activities aren't typically their first priority while drinking and using—so you might want to take it slow and not turn this into a chore or a "should" that sets your PIR up for failure. It's probably best with some PIRs to make it a natural part of learning to have fun, something we talk about later in this chapter, as opposed to being a strict regimen they will have a hard time adhering to. Still, almost all my PIR friends (and both former boyfriends) work out in the gym. Mark, Frank, Paul, Sandy, and Bob are diligent about maintaining their physical health and are in great shape. Treadmills, cycling, and other aerobic exercises, as well as lifting weights, are wonderful for increasing endorphin levels in the brain, rebuilding muscle mass, and strengthening muscles that have been weakened by years of disuse. If you are a dedicated "gym rat" and your PIR is too, you could consider working out together if your schedules and types of workouts permit it.

PIRs are often encouraged to do various forms of stretching exercises to help alleviate body tension. Techniques like yoga or tai chi can be a great way to not only stretch the body, but to focus the mind as well because of the concentration it takes to do the exercises involved in such programs. This focus doesn't just help retrain brain circuits; it helps practitioners stay in the moment, as they become aware of their surroundings and appreciate merely "being." When was the last time you slowed down, stretched, or meditated? You and your PIR could have a great time taking a class together. If either or both of you haven't done this type of exercise before, I suggest starting with something that is easy on the body, like a simple version of tai chi or gentle yoga.

Walking and hiking are also good opportunities for both PIRs and their partners to "smell the roses." Remembering to stay in the moment while walking can benefit the soul as well as the body. My friends Seth and Pam, who take regular walks around their neighborhood, told me that such strolls are ways to savor their moments together and chances to reconnect and "debrief" at the end of a day.

Another good form of exercise for PIRs and non-PIRs is swimming. There is something about trusting the water to support one's body that is very comforting—especially to those fairly new to recovery for whom trust is a huge issue. Bicycling is great exercise as well. (Try riding a tandem bike with your PIR, and take turns riding in front. It's a wonderful way to practice trusting and letting go of control!) Then there's my favorite exercise: good old running—a great endorphin producer, provided your PIR's body can handle it and neither of you have knee or hip problems. My PIR neighbor Tom is a runner and is very dedicated to his exercise. He belongs to a running club and competes in marathons. He and his longtime partner Alex (also a PIR) and I often make a habit of walking our dogs together through the neighborhood—which is good exercise for humans and canines alike!

There are so many benefits to exercise—it reduces tension, helps one sleep better, elevates one's mood, and can contribute to a more positive body image. Exercise can also be a fun and rewarding way for PIRs and their partners to spend time together in a healthy way that doesn't have anything to do with alcohol or drugs. As with anyone starting an exercise program, PIRs *and* their partners should remember "Easy does it"—start slowly and gradually with any exercise program. Ideally, like proper nutrition, exercise will become a part of a balanced and positive lifestyle for both of you.

Even though they're learning to take better care of their bodies, your PIR may still have a few unhealthy habits—like

smoking. Smoking is very, very common for those in recovery. I have had to walk through many a cloud of smoke
when attending certain Twelve Step events, or upon entering a building in which a recovery meeting is going on.
Virtually all of my PIRs and PIR friends smoked during
their recovery. Some stopped within a year of recovery;
some within five years; and some still smoke. Many famous
PIRs smoked, including Bill Wilson, who died as a result of
heavy smoking. Nicotine has long been recognized as an addictive drug, and more and more addiction counselors are
taking the stance that the PIR has not been fully successful in their recovery unless they not only quit drinking and
drugging, but they quit smoking as well. Smoking is often
more accepted in early recovery, as the school of thought is
"pick your poisons"—at least the PIR is sober from alcohol
and drugs. But once the PIR has a solid grasp of their program, they are urged to lay off the tobacco as well, as part of
their healthy lifestyle in recovery.

Many PIRs who are addicted to nicotine actually find it
easier to quit everything at once, because for so many the
ritual of smoking went hand in hand with using alcohol
and other drugs. For them, lighting up a cigarette can still
trigger the urge to drink or take drugs.

There are so many valid reasons to quit using nicotine—
risk of various cancers, inhalation of secondhand smoke
by friends and loved ones, the money one spends on cigarettes, the smelly clothes, the diminished sense of taste and
smell. But my friends Tom and Alex also pointed out to
me something I hadn't realized—that nicotine can affect
your mind and emotions as well. Alex thinks nicotine addiction is worse than alcohol or drug addiction—he says

you suppress your emotions by smoking. After he quit, he said his sensitivity level was so high that he cried for three months. It was only after he quit smoking that he realized what an emotional crutch smoking had been for him. He had quit for a long time in his sobriety, but then his former partner passed away and the stress of this made him start again. He says this second time was even worse, with more of a need to smoke and then worse withdrawal symptoms. Tom quit smoking about five years ago, and Alex laughingly reminded him, "You were crazy when you quit! Remember we got you knitting needles because you were so nervous?" We all had a good laugh about this, picturing Tom knitting at breakneck speed.

Your PIR may very well still be a smoker, and that will be a big consideration for you if you are a nonsmoker and want to continue your relationship. My PIR Steve was wearing a patch when I met him, but had gone back to smoking about four months into our relationship. It annoyed me, but at least he was careful not to smoke around me, and he wore a clean shirt if we were going out somewhere. By that point, I was smitten with him and kept dating him despite his smoking, but I don't know if I could have tolerated it for the long term. (More about that in the next chapter.)

In addition to good nutrition, a regular exercise program, and a healthy lifestyle, the PIRs I know said they also had to relearn how to have fun. For them, fun used to involve using or drinking. It can take practice to learn how to enjoy oneself without using mind-altering chemicals. Having fun, laughing, and playing are all ways to stimulate the brain to produce dopamine, just like exercise does. It is important to get dopamine and other feel-good chemicals flowing naturally through the brain, because without it PIRs can feel uncomfortable and may want to use again. Just like exercise, learning how to have fun in a healthy way is something a PIR works on one day at a time. Being able to take things lightly and laugh at oneself is good for anyone. Remember Rule #9, "Don't take yourself so damn seriously"? Not taking oneself so seriously is a very positive practice. As previously mentioned, there is a lot of laughter in Twelve Step meetings, as PIRs gradually learn to open up and enjoy themselves—and this lightheartedness can carry over into other relationships. One time my friend Mark took a group of us to a local comedy club and we laughed ourselves crazy, PIRs and non-PIRs alike. Watching funny movies, going to funny musicals or theater productions—all of this can help PIRs and their partners share in fun and laughter.

In the first couple years of recovery, it's important for PIRs to get out, keep busy, and do healthy things to fill the time gaps that used to be filled by drinking or using. There are many fun activities that you and your PIR could enjoy as you both practice living a healthy lifestyle. My PIR loved outdoor activities. We went to outdoor festivals and markets on the weekends. He also loved to go to garage sales on Saturday mornings. Other fun things to do could include:

- going to artsy places, like museums, art galleries, craft fairs, outdoor art festivals, or antique malls
- going to entertainment venues, like theatrical productions, comedy clubs, concerts (outside or inside), or coffeehouses
- going to parks, such as amusement parks, state parks, dog parks, meditation gardens, flower shows, or historic parks and venues

- participating in other forms of exercise not already mentioned, like playing tennis, racquetball, volleyball, horseback riding, fishing, skiing, or golfing

Every couple is different, and everyone has their own likes, dislikes, and energy levels, regardless of whether or not they are in recovery. Again, just be open and honest with your date, and encourage them to be honest with you as well. My neighbors Tom (sober ten years) and Alex (sober twenty-three years) have different energy levels and skills. For exercise, Alex, who is more laid-back, likes tennis, whereas Tom is a marathon runner, as previously mentioned. Together, though, they do many fun things, such as taking their dogs to the dog park and socializing with other owners there. They told me that it's hard for a PIR in the gay community to meet potential partners, as gay culture is so tied into going to bars and nightclubs. They often go to events sponsored by their local "gay AA" group. In fact, the two of them met at an AA-sponsored country line dance (Alex is an avid dancer). Mostly, though, they hang out with their straight friends—they think it's funny that I, being in theater, have more gay friends than they do! They love cruises, but prefer the "regular" cruises, Tom said, not the gay-themed ones, as they think the latter are more geared for singles looking to meet others and can be quite the "meat markets." Alex's passion is antiques. He is an antiques dealer and frequently shops at antique fairs and markets. Tom and Alex have been together happily for nine years. Tom was only nine months sober when they met, and would only participate in AA-sponsored activities at the time, as he didn't feel safe or ready to meet anyone outside of the program. Even though they consider themselves homebodies at this point in their lives, they strongly suggest AA- and NA-sponsored events for PIRs and their partners, because they're fun and there isn't any tension around alcohol or other drug use.

When I was dating Steve, we attended several parties that were hosted by the owner of the sober house where Steve had previously lived. I found out that there are many AA- and NA-sponsored activities that couples can participate in. The easiest and most obvious are the open meetings. These are very enlightening for someone outside the program—you get to see and hear firsthand what your PIR has talked about, and you will learn along with your PIR. Sober events that cater to those in recovery also abound in many cities. Your PIR may already have a list of these or have ideas about where to go. It is fun to be out and socializing with others of like mind. If you progress in your relationship and begin to spend a lot of time with your PIR, there are also Twelve Step–themed retreats, conventions, and special package deals you can try out, with everything from rafting trips to Club Med–type vacations. You can have fun on sober cruises, tours, and vacations all over the world.

Even if you may have had trepidations about dating a PIR and all that it entails, I know from personal experience that it is very freeing to date someone who does not drink or use. You know that if they like you, they like you with a clear mind—there are no substances to influence their opinion of you. When they go to events with you, they remember names, details, and conversations. And you do not have to be the designated driver! Many choices of where to go and what to eat are actually simpler if you date a PIR, and many of these choices are also healthier. Joining together in exercise, having fun outdoors, and even just talking together can be easy choices to make. Your PIR may also be more open to your beliefs about spirituality, or at least be willing to discuss the similarities and differences in your respective beliefs. Dating someone who is a "work in progress," who is continuing to work on and improve him- or herself, is a tremendous opportunity for growth on both of your parts, and for your relationship. I have learned a lot since the early days of dating my PIRs, and much of what I learned was, ironically, about my own self. And for that, I'm extremely grateful.

[12]

Some Things to Consider If the Relationship Gets Serious

WHEN MY RELATIONSHIP with Steve ended, I was thrown for a loop for quite a while. It took some time before I could even think about dating, let alone consider dating anyone in recovery. Profiles of men would pop up on my dating website, and if I saw that they didn't drink, I'd give them a wide berth—I didn't even bother to find out their reasons. About a year later when I started writing this book and began interviewing non-PIR spouses or partners of PIRs, I confess that I thought they must be a little crazy. Who in their right mind would be in a long-term relationship with a PIR? And why would they stay in such a relationship?

Well, first of all, there is the highly significant "L" word. Every one of these PIR partners was deeply in love with their PIR. It's true that love can be blind, but these PIR partners were so much in love with their PIR that they had taken a good, hard, honest look at their potential mates prior to long-term commitment, and decided "aye" rather than "nay." They were able to see the person beyond the disease. They could see addiction for what it was—a chronic, treatable disease. They ultimately made the decision to be with their partners despite the knowledge that their PIRs would be addressing this disease for the rest of their lives. Some PIR partners even swear that PIRs make better spouses because of all the "soul" work they've done and how they've learned to take responsibility for their own behavior. And guess what? These couples are still together, and their relationships are stronger than ever. Of course, I had the good fortune to interview couples who are in healthy relationships. I am well aware that there are also unhealthy partnerships with PIRs, and I did my share of talking to some of these people too. But when you factor in the odds these days of any two people staying in a long-term relationship (we hear that one of every two marriages ends in divorce), I think PIR partnerships are doing pretty well.

There are many things to consider if you and your PIR get serious and start to think long-term. As with any relationship, both partners come to the table with baggage from past relationships or experiences. However, you may have just a carry-on, whereas your PIR may have several suitcases! (Or the opposite could be true—I've known several PIR partners with their own heavy loads.) One example from your PIR's past might be a pissed-off ex-partner. Maybe the partnership broke up due to your PIR's drinking or using, and now his or her ex may be even angrier because their ex, now clean and sober, is having a good relationship with you, the new person. They might feel resentment at how "easy" you must have it now compared to what they went through. And they would probably have good reason to think that! Would *you* have wanted to be involved with your PIR back when they were using? To understand where your PIR's ex is coming from, remember from a previous chapter that addiction takes its toll on all members of the family, but especially the spouse. And remember that due to the spouse's coping efforts, he or she may develop behaviors similar to their addicted partner. They may deny that anything's wrong; they may lie or make excuses for the addict; they may even blame themselves—all in an effort to control something that is beyond their ability to manage. Their life gradually spirals out of control, just like their addictive partner's life did. If the marriage or relationship ends and the ex-partner does not seek help getting their own life back together, he or she may hang on to resentments for years and years. I saw this during the time I spent in Al-Anon, which is an excellent place for learning to put the focus back on *you,* as opposed to the addict, in order to move on into the future. If you do come up against an angry ex, the only thing you can do is acknowledge their feelings and remember there are two sides to every story—everyone may still be hurting, and this is not a good place for anyone to be. Then you gently step back and remind yourself that "you didn't cause it, you can't cure it, and you can't control it."

You may also be in contact with your PIR's children from a previous marriage or relationship. Adding children to the equation can be tricky, even in a relationship without addiction. The stakes are higher when the children are the product of an addictive, dysfunctional family. Children from addictive families can have many emotional issues of their own. They, too, developed coping skills that can mimic addictive behavior. A child may have grown used to lying and covering up for the addictive parent; blaming him- or herself for the parent's addiction; or manipulating other family members and friends in an effort to "help" the parent.

Depending on many factors, such as how old the child was when the addiction became a problem or how the non-addictive parent reacted, a child from an addictive family may either do fairly well once the parent is in recovery, or may have a hard time adjusting to this new reality. The child may harbor resentments aimed at the PIR parent. And, because of the nature of addiction, he or she is also at much greater risk for becoming an addict.

Your PIR may have already done a lot of work to rebuild trust and healing with his or her children. If they are still working on this, you may be indirectly involved in the process. Some of my PIR-partner friends did encounter resentments and dysfunction in their PIR's children. My friend Grace met her future husband, Joe, when he had ten years of sobriety. She came to find out that Joe's oldest son had not spoken to him for many years. Grace realized she couldn't repair the breach in that relationship. It was not her fault nor part of her history, so she stepped out of the equation, being supportive of her PIR, but letting him work to heal the relationship with his son. On the other hand, the son of my friend Joan's PIR doesn't have any of these issues. He is just sixteen and his father has been sober and doing well in recovery for fourteen years, so he never really knew his "using" dad. Joan and Jack have been diligent about watching out for Jack's son, monitoring his school activities and social life, and are not making any permanent changes in residency until he graduates from high school.

My friends Donna and Frank had a situation that was a middle ground between these two examples. Donna had been married for fourteen years to a cocaine addict. (She dryly says, "I seem to attract addicts.") Donna's daughter was sixteen when Donna and Frank met. Kristy was "a hellacious teenager," not nice to Frank at all. What helped turn her daughter around was that she saw how kindly Frank treated Donna. "He stayed by my side," Donna explained. Kristy highly valued how hard Frank was working in his recovery, and how loyal he was to her mom. In seeing the good example that Frank set with her mom, Kristy was able to move beyond her distrust of yet another addict in her life. She and Frank are now "best friends," and she is proud to call him her stepfather.

As challenging as it might be for you to deal with your PIR's history and family, your own family members may also have a hard time if you become serious with your PIR, because of the stigma still associated with addiction. I remember when I first started dating Steve. It took a while before I was able to tell my parents that he was a PIR. I took it nice and slow, and didn't give them too much information all at once. I just calmly explained about AA and the hard work that PIRs do in a recovery program. My dad happened to have known a work colleague in our hometown who had been in AA for quite some time. This gentleman was a shining example of Step Twelve—he was stalwart in his program and regularly extended his hand to other addicts through outreach and service. Through knowing him, Dad came to realize the good that can happen when someone sincerely follows a Twelve Step program. This seemed to lessen my parents' anxiety that I was dating a PIR, and I silently sent thanks to this guy whom I didn't know, but instantly respected!

I found out that some partners of PIRs didn't fare as well as I did when it came to sharing their dating news with their families. Because of a long history of alcoholism in my friend Pam's family, her mother was "terrified" when she started dating Seth. Pam told me that it personally never bothered her, as she never equated Seth in his recovery with her alcoholic relatives who were not in recovery. Her mom eventually came around and grew to accept and respect Seth when she saw how hard he worked—and lived—his recovery program. My friend Grace's father was an alcoholic who finally started going to AA just two years before he died, so her family was understandably concerned when Grace met and married her PIR, Joe. Because Grace attended Al-Anon and also a Twelve Step codependency group, she felt better prepared to deal with issues regarding her relationship with Joe *and* her family's concerns about her dating a PIR.

Donna's parents were alcoholics, and she was sent to live with a foster mother at age sixteen. Her biological mother had another child, and this half-sister is also an alcoholic. Donna said she is "amazed" that she is not an addict herself; however, she is well aware, as are Pam and Grace, that because of her family history, she "attracted" a PIR, as do many adult children of alcoholics. These women also know that many adult children of addicts may commit to a serious relationship with a PIR in order to fix or change them—to complete the job that they could not do with their parents. Pam, Grace, and Donna realize that because of their addictive family history, they have some codependent tendencies, and have learned to monitor themselves—and their relationships with their PIRs—accordingly.

It helps very much when both families of the couple are loving and accepting, and I was pleased to discover that so many families of the people I interviewed were just that.

My friends Tom and Alex are fortunate that their families are supportive of their relationship *and* their respective recovery programs. Tom frequently spends time with his extended family in the Midwest, and Alex's dad lives here in our area.

Another issue to consider if you're thinking long-term with your PIR is finances. As touched on in other chapters, money and differing styles of handling money are some of the top causes of stress in a marriage or serious relationship. The stakes are upped if you're in a relationship with a PIR who may still have outstanding debts from their past. If you marry your PIR, you might also become responsible for these debts, depending on the laws in your particular state. Your PIR may owe years of child support or your PIR could still be attempting to resolve their credit history. I urge you to honestly and lovingly discuss these matters with your PIR before they become huge issues and areas of tension. You may need the help of a professional—an attorney or a financial advisor—to help clarify the money situation, to protect yourself, and to set up a solid financial plan for the both of you.

Hopefully, as part of their solid recovery program, your PIR is working to establish a good plan for their future health. However, they may have past health issues related to addiction, some of which may warrant consideration in a long-term relationship. Drinking or using can block the addict's inhibitions, wipe out their judgment, and increase their sex drive. As a result, alcoholics and drug addicts are at risk for sexually transmitted diseases (STDs) due to increased promiscuity, unprotected sex, and weakened immune systems, all as a result of their addiction. It is a good idea for both you and your PIR to be tested for STDs before you make any decisions about long-term commitments. And when you do, make sure you get tested for HIV/AIDS. The AIDS (acquired immune deficiency syndrome) virus can be spread by contaminated needles as well as by unprotected sex. Intravenous drug users are especially at risk, so keep that in mind if your PIR used heroin or some other drug that users often "shoot up" for a faster and more intense high. If you or your partner is a gay male and one or both of you are PIRs, the risk for HIV/AIDS is even greater. The point is, all sexually active couples—regardless of their drug-using history—should get tested for STDs before proceeding with a sexual relationship. Even if you or your PIR has not had sex for a while, there is still the possibility that STDs can be transmitted because certain viruses can lie dormant in a person's system for years.

Other health issues down the road that your PIR may have to monitor are liver disease (although most liver disease is reversible with sobriety), gastrointestinal problems, and a weakened skeletal system due to a lack of calcium absorption. Your PIR may also have a smoker's cough and other respiratory health problems down the road if they are addicted to nicotine and/or marijuana, especially if they continue to smoke cigarettes or use other forms of tobacco. As mentioned in chapter 11, many PIRs smoke for years in sobriety. Those who have kicked the habit can tell you that nicotine addiction is one of the hardest of all addictions to quit. Even with the new "e-cigarettes" that don't have a tobacco odor, your PIR is still inhaling nicotine. Is this something you can deal with in the long term? My friend Alex says that his partner, Tom, is now so much healthier emotionally, as well as physically, since he quit nicotine. As mentioned previously, Alex considers smoking to be an emotional crutch. If nicotine use is an issue for you, you may want to honestly consider if you want a relationship with a PIR who is endangering their health (and yours), and who might be stuffing their emotions because of a nicotine addiction. If you are the smoker and your PIR does not smoke, I encourage you to have an honest discussion with him or her to explore how your addiction may be affecting them and their recovery.

Other emotional issues that may linger in sobriety could be ongoing anxiety and panic attacks, as it may take years before the PIR's moods are stabilized. If your PIR has a moody personality to begin with, like my friend Frank does, you need to think long and hard if this is something that meshes with your own personality in the long run. Frank and Donna work well together because Donna is emotionally the opposite of Frank; she takes things lightly, whereas he has a tendency to be very serious. What about you? Do you shake off other people's moods, or do you tend to absorb them? Are you a person who lets things bounce off you, or are you a thinker and a brooder? Now is the time to examine your own self and try to see if, in the long run, you and your PIR will complement—or sabotage—each other emotionally.

As was discussed in chapter 8, many PIRs have other mental health disorders such as depression, obsessive-compulsive disorder (OCD), bipolar disorder, or post-traumatic stress disorder (PTSD). I know from living with people who have these disorders how tricky it can be to treat the disorder. Medications on their own do not always produce the results either of you want, or they may have unsatisfactory side effects. The best treatment is usually a combination of behavioral and cognitive therapy, medication, and lifestyle changes such as good nutrition, exercise, and stress management. My marriage suffered because of my spouse's depression. My friend Mark occasionally still struggles with depression and bipolar disorder. If your PIR has a mental illness, make sure they are doing everything they can to manage it, much like they are managing their addiction disorder, or it may eventually start to take a toll on your relationship.

In the early days of gathering information for this book, I had a little questionnaire that I used when I interviewed my PIR friends and partners of PIRs. I had them check boxes next to the traits that the PIRs were still exhibiting in recovery. Almost all of them checked the boxes next to low self-esteem, hypersensitivity, and perfectionism. These may not seem like relationship killers, but a combination of the three could slowly drive you nuts as the years go by. One of my PIR-partner friends said that her PIR's low self-esteem resulted in them not having enough money in certain months to pay their bills. Her PIR would greatly undercharge his customers for his services because he didn't think he was worthy of getting paid. This became an ongoing source of frustration for her, and they eventually had to go to counseling for it. One of my PIR friends is a perfectionist and confessed that it disturbs him when things are not in proper order in his house; he has to battle his perfectionism constantly so that he doesn't upset his wife. Another PIR partner said that her husband is very sensitive to change, and they are living in the same house they bought years ago even though they would save a lot of money by downsizing. These examples are not life-or-death issues, but now is the time to examine them and honestly ask yourself if they would bother you in the long run.

Remember the description from chapter 5, "big egos with an inferiority complex inside"? Many PIRs, including several of my friends who have been in recovery for years, have worked hard on their egos and grandiosity tendencies, but they still have rather dominant personalities. You know right away when they're in a room, as they tend to take over a crowd. It's not usually in an obnoxious way—they actually can be very funny and charming. Your PIR may be one of these types, and if you are okay with it, that's terrific. Several PIR partners I know tend to be introverted, quiet, and sweet, and the balance between them and their partners is perfect— they truly complement each other. Personally, in my choice of men, someone with a big ego or a dominating personality doesn't work for me, as I too have a dominant personality and it's too much of a clash. It could be my theater background, but I enjoy working the crowd and being funny. Through the study of spiritual materials and books, I have done a lot of work on my own ego, to make sure that it doesn't crave drama or rule my emotions. Sometimes, though, I will still react strongly to another person's ego, and I now know enough to recognize that this situation is just two egos re- acting to each other. Anyway, even with all my awareness of this, I am still not evolved enough to be comfortable with someone who has a big ego, let alone be in a long-term re- lationship with him. Sooner is better than later in knowing these things about yourself when it comes to making long- term commitments. It may be time for you, too, to examine your ego and your PIR's ego and see if they can get along!

Along those lines, PIRs are always supposed to put their sobriety first, and even if they've worked on their ego, they will always continue to monitor and check on themselves if they're committed to working their recovery program. If you truly support their recovery efforts, you must be okay with that. It (recovery) will always "be about them," but relationships are still about balance and require a healthy give-and-take. So if you're thinking about taking your relationship to a deeper, more serious level, ask yourself honestly if your PIR supports you emotionally, as you support them. These are all important things to consider before you take the relationship plunge.

My friend Seth has very honestly told me what has worked and what hasn't in his long marriage to Pam, some of which you've already read about in this book. One of his challenges is taking on too much and being involved in too many things, and he has learned to take a step back when that happens. He is also aware that he might go into a dark, moody place for brief periods of time, but he's learned to talk to Pam about what's going on when he starts to feel depressed, and to work through his feelings with her help. He says, "When you are helpmates with someone you deeply love, you each still have remnants of your old self. You know your old self will come out now and again, and you accept that and move through it." Pam agrees, and adds that she didn't realize Seth was "so serious" when she'd first met him. She has worked on lightening up the marriage, adding humor and laughter. They have their own personal little signals that they use with each other when they're around other people, such as winking or tugging on their ear, to keep them in touch with each other and to stay connected in the midst of others. Theirs is a solid partnership that has lasted for thirty-eight years.

Although they haven't been together as long as Seth and Pam, Frank and Donna also continue to do well in their relationship. Donna deals with Frank's moods by "knowing and reminding myself, at the end of the day, that this has nothing to do with me." The most important things in their relationship are honesty and trust. After Donna's dysfunctional past relationships, this trust is something new, positive, and very important for her to experience with her PIR.

Alex says that in his long-term relationship with Tom, it is important to make amends; it doesn't matter who's right or who's wrong—eventually that isn't what's really important. Tom says that he takes comfort in knowing that Alex is there for him and is such a wonderful helpmate, who does for him "beyond what I can do for myself." Tom constantly reminds himself that PIRs are not famous for being good at relationships. If he reacts too quickly to a situation and is about to say something hurtful, he reminds himself, "You're not the best-skilled at this," and he takes a moment to regroup. He appreciates Alex all the more because Alex is better at handling his emotions, although Alex admits that he can be somewhat blunt at times. It is obvious that they both have great respect and love for each other. Their understanding of each other has increased with time, and, as they both say, they have "bonded as one."

These couples are examples of successful long-term, committed relationships that can happen if one or both of the partners are in recovery. I hope you are as heartened as I was by hearing the stories of how, with hard work, love, and trust in each other and their Higher Powers, their relationships not only survived—they flourished. The words I kept hearing as I spoke with these partners were: *honesty, trust, respect,* and *love.* I found the answer to my question. *This* is how someone can stay in a relationship with a PIR: by both partners practicing these principles daily—principles they learned not *in spite* of recovery, but *because* of it.

I have certainly learned a lot in my quest for knowledge about PIRs and their partners. I understand more clearly what happened in my own relationships with my PIRs—what worked and why it worked, and what ultimately went wrong. I am better prepared for future relationships, especially if those partnerships are with a PIR, and I more fully appreciate how the principles of recovery can help both of us get the most out of such a relationship.

I hope that you have learned something too. It is my sincere wish that the knowledge you have gained from this book will help you in your journey with your PIR, whether you're on your first date or your fiftieth. So I leave you with the same wish with which I began: Blessings on your journey!

Notes

1. Betty Ford Center, "Betty Ford Institute," *BFC Insights,* June 1, 2007, http://www.bettyfordcenter.org/recovery/methods -techniques/betty-ford-institute.php.

2. *Alcoholics Anonymous,* 4th ed. (New York: Alcoholics Anonymous World Services, 2001), xiii.

3. "Jim's Story," in *Alcoholics Anonymous,* 4th ed. (New York: Alcoholics Anonymous World Services, 2001), 232–45.

4. "The Housewife Who Drank at Home," in *Alcoholics Anonymous,* 4th ed. (New York: Alcoholics Anonymous World Services, 2001), 295–300.

5. "Listening to the Wind," in *Alcoholics Anonymous,* 4th ed. (New York: Alcoholics Anonymous World Services, 2001), 458–69.

6. "One Third Step for Me, One Giant Leap for My Recovery," in *Narcotics Anonymous,* 6th ed. (Van Nuys, CA: Narcotics Anonymous World Services, 2008), 240–44.

7. "A Quiet Satisfaction," in *Narcotics Anonymous,* 6th ed. (Van Nuys, CA: Narcotics Anonymous World Services, 2008), 179–83.

8. "Restored to Dignity," in *Narcotics Anonymous,* 6th ed. (Van Nuys, CA: Narcotics Anonymous World Services, 2008), 187–91.

9. National Institute on Drug Abuse, *Drugs, Brains, and Behavior: The Science of Addiction,* NIH pub. number: 10-5605 (Bethesda, MD: National Institute on Drug Abuse, 2007, revised 2010), 5, www.drugabuse.gov/sites/default/files/sciofaddiction.pdf.

10. *Alcoholics Anonymous,* 4th ed., xxviii.

11. National Institute on Drug Abuse, *Drugs, Brains, and Behavior, 5.*

12. *Alcoholics Anonymous,* 4th ed., 336.

13. The Twelve Steps are from *Alcoholics Anonymous,* 4th ed., 59–60.

14. *Alcoholics Anonymous,* 4th ed., 77–78.

15. Ibid., 78.

16. Bill W., "The Next Frontier: Emotional Sobriety," *AA Grapevine* (Jan. 1958).

17. Ibid.

18. *Alcoholics Anonymous,* 4th ed., 89.

19. Bill W., "The Next Frontier: Emotional Sobriety."

20. *Alcoholics Anonymous,* 4th ed., 9.

21. The King James version of this prayer is "Our Father, which art in Heaven/Hallowed be thy name./Thy kingdom come/Thy will be done in earth/As it is in Heaven./Give us this day our daily bread,/and forgive us our debts, as we forgive our debtors./And lead us not into temptation,/but deliver us from evil./For thine is the kingdom,/and the power, and the glory, forever./Amen."

22. Robert Frost, "The Road Not Taken," in *Mountain Interval* (New York: Henry Holt and Company, 1916), reprinted in *The Road Not Taken and Other Poems* (Mineola, NY: Dover Publications, 1993).

23. Ernest Hemingway, *A Farewell to Arms* (New York: Charles Scribner's Sons, 1929).

24. *Alcoholics Anonymous,* 4th ed., 101.

Bibliography

Adams, A. J. *Undrunk: A Skeptic's Guide to AA.* Center City, MN: Hazelden, 2009.

Alcoholics Anonymous. 4th ed. New York: Alcoholics Anonymous World Services, 2001.

Al-Anon's Twelve Steps & Twelve Traditions. Rev. ed. Virginia Beach, VA: Al-Anon Family Group Headquarters, 2005.

American Psychiatric Association. *Diagnostic and Statistical Manual of Mental Disorders.* 5th ed. Arlington, VA: American Psychiatric Association, 2013.

Beattie, Melody. *Codependent No More: How to Stop Controlling Others and Start Caring for Yourself.* Center City, MN: Hazelden, 1986.

———. *The Language of Letting Go: Daily Meditations on Codependency.* Center City, MN: Hazelden, 1990.

Berger, Allen. *12 Smart Things to Do When the Booze and Drugs Are Gone: Choosing Emotional Sobriety through Self-Awareness and Right Action.* Center City, MN: Hazelden, 2010.

Betty Ford Center. "Betty Ford Institute." *BFC Insights,* June 1, 2007. http://www.bettyfordcenter.org/recovery/methods-techniques /betty-ford-institute.php.

Betty Ford Institute Consensus Panel. "What Is Recovery? A Working Definition from the Betty Ford Institute." *Journal of Substance Abuse Treatment* 33 (2007): 221–28.

Came to Believe. New York: Alcoholics Anonymous World Services, 1973.

Cohen, Sidney. *The Chemical Brain: The Neurochemistry of Addictive Disorders.* Irvine, CA: Care Institute, 1988.

Conyers, Beverly. *Everything Changes: Help for Families of Newly Recovering Addicts.* Center City, MN: Hazelden, 2009.

Courage to Change: One Day at a Time in Al-Anon II. Virginia Beach, VA: Al-Anon Family Group Headquarters, 1992.

Daley, Dennis C. *Kicking Addictive Habits Once and for All: A Relapse-Prevention Guide.* San Francisco, CA: Jossey-Bass, 1991.

Diamond, Jonathan. *Narrative Means to Sober Ends: Treating Addiction and Its Aftermath.* New York: Guilford Press, 2000.

Dyer, Wayne W. *The Power of Intention: Learning to Co-create Your World Your Way.* Carlsbad, CA: Hay House, 2004.

F., Dan. *Sober but Stuck: Obstacles Most Often Encountered That Keep Us from Growing in Recovery.* Center City, MN: Hazelden, 1991.

Faulkner, Mary. *Easy Does It Dating Guide: For People in Recovery.* Center City, MN: Hazelden, 2004.

———. *Easy Does It Relationship Guide: For People in Recovery.* Center City, MN: Hazelden, 2007.

Frost, Robert. "The Road Not Taken." In *Mountain Interval.* New York: Henry Holt and Company, 1916. Reprinted in *The Road Not Taken and Other Poems.* Mineola, NY: Dover Publications, 1993.

Gorski, Terence T. *Passages through Recovery: An Action Plan for Preventing Relapse.* Center City, MN: Hazelden, 1989.

Gorski, Terence T., and Merlene Miller. *Staying Sober: A Guide for Relapse Prevention.* Independence, MO: Herald House/Independence Press, 1986.

Hemingway, Ernest. *A Farewell to Arms.* New York: Charles Scribner's Sons, 1929.

Kettelhack, Guy. *Sober and Free: Making Your Recovery Work for You.* New York: Fireside, 1996.

Living Sober. New York: Alcoholics Anonymous World Services, 1998.

Miller, Merlene, Terence Gorski, and David K. Miller. *Learning to Live Again: A Guide for Recovery from Chemical Dependency.* Independence, MO: Herald House/Independence Press, 1992.

Mooney, Al J., Arlene Eisenberg, and Howard Eisenberg. *The Recovery Book.* New York: Workman Publishing, 1992.

Mulford, Harold A. "Stages in the Alcoholic Process: Toward a Cumulative, Nonsequential Index." *Journal of Studies on Alcohol* 38, no. 3 (1977): 563–83.

Nakken, Craig. *The Addictive Personality: Understanding the Addictive Process and Compulsive Behavior.* Center City, MN: Hazelden, 1996.

Narcotics Anonymous. 6th ed. Van Nuys, CA: Narcotics Anonymous World Services, 2008.

National Institute on Drug Abuse. *Drugs, Brains, and Behavior: The Science of Addiction.* NIH pub. number: 10-5605. Bethesda, MD: National Institute on Drug Abuse, 2007, revised 2010.

Rogers, Ronald L., and Chandler Scott McMillin. *Relapse Traps: How to Avoid the 12 Most Common Pitfalls in Recovery.* New York: Bantam, 1991.

Tolle, Eckhart. *A New Earth: Awakening to Your Life's Purpose.* New York: Penguin Group, 2006.

Twelve Steps and Twelve Traditions. New York: Alcoholics Anonymous World Services, 1981.

Twerski, Abraham J. *Addictive Thinking: Understanding Self-Deception.* 2nd ed. Center City, MN: Hazelden, 1997.

W., Bill. "The Next Frontier: Emotional Sobriety." *AA Grapevine,* Jan. 1958.

West, James W. *The Betty Ford Center Book of Answers.* New York: Simon and Schuster, 1997.

About the Author

Karen Nagy lives and works in South Florida, having moved there many years ago from her hometown in western Pennsylvania. She has a master's degree in music theater and has been seen onstage as a singer and actor, in the pit as a musician, or backstage as a technician in theaters throughout South Florida. She is a proud member of AEA (Actors' Equity Association), NATS (National Association of Teachers of Singing), and NSAI (Nashville Songwriters Association International). She teaches voice, music theater, sightsinging, and music appreciation at the college level. Karen has sung, played, or music-directed in churches and synagogues since the age of seven, and each experience has brought her further on her own spiritual path. Karen's passions are therapy-dog work, sea turtle rescue, golf, and the Steelers.

Hazelden, a national nonprofit organization founded in 1949, helps people reclaim their lives from the disease of addiction. Built on decades of knowledge and experience, Hazelden offers a comprehensive approach to addiction that addresses the full range of patient, family, and professional needs, including treatment and continuing care for youth and adults, research, higher learning, public education and advocacy, and publishing.

A life of recovery is lived "one day at a time." Hazelden publications, both educational and inspirational, support and strengthen lifelong recovery. In 1954, Hazelden published *Twenty-Four Hours a Day,* the first daily meditation book for recovering alcoholics, and Hazelden continues to publish works to inspire and guide individuals in treatment and recovery, and their loved ones. Professionals who work to prevent and treat addiction also turn to Hazelden for evidence-based curricula, informational materials, and videos for use in schools, treatment programs, and correctional programs.

Through published works, Hazelden extends the reach of hope, encouragement, help, and support to individuals, families, and communities affected by addiction and related issues.

For questions about Hazelden publications, please call **800-328-9000** or visit us online at **hazelden.org/bookstore.**

Other titles that may interest you:

Undrunk
A Skeptic's Guide to AA
A. J. Adams
> Adams uses self-deprecating humor, entertaining anecdotes, and frank descriptions to introduce anyone who "just doesn't get" Alcoholics Anonymous to the complete "Undrunk" lifestyle.

Order No. 2944 (softcover), EB2944 (e-book)

Everything Changes
Help for Families of Newly Recovering Addicts
Beverly Conyers
> *Everything Changes* assuages fears and uncertainty by teaching loved ones of newly recovering addicts how to navigate the often-tumultuous early months of recovery.

Order No. 3807 (softcover), EB3807 (e-book)

Codependent No More
How to Stop Controlling Others and Start Caring for Yourself
Melody Beattie
> The healing touchstone of millions, this modern classic holds the key to understanding codependency and to unlocking its stultifying hold on your life.

Order No. 5014 (softcover), EB5014 (e-book)

Hazelden books are available at fine bookstores everywhere. To order from Hazelden, call **800-328-9000** or visit **hazelden .org/bookstore.**